The
ESTHETIC INTENT
of
TIECK'S
FANTASTIC COMEDY

The

ESTHETIC INTENT

of

TIECK'S
FANTASTIC COMEDY

By

RAYMOND M. IMMERWAHR

ASSOCIATE PROFESSOR OF GERMAN

WASHINGTON UNIVERSITY

WASHINGTON UNIVERSITY STUDIES — NEW SERIES

LANGUAGE AND LITERATURE—No. 22

SAINT LOUIS, 1953

ٺ

PREFACE

The studies resulting in the following pages began under the stimulating direction of Professor Edward V. Brewer as research for a doctoral dissertation submitted in 1941 at the University of California. The interruption of the war years made it necessary to begin this research virtually afresh, but its completion was expedited by a grant from Washington University in the summer of 1950. While some parts of the present monograph may be considered a thoroughgoing revision of the dissertation, others are entirely new, and so also is the focus upon fantastic comedy.

In so far as the intervening years may have resulted in a clearer and more mature perspective, credit is due in very large part to the intellectual stimulus and heightened awareness of literary values I have received from my colleagues at Washington University, and in particular to the challenging criticism of Professor Fred O. Nolte. My thanks are also due to him and to the other scholars who have read my manuscript for invaluable suggestions to improve its presentation and accuracy: Professor Brewer, Professor Erich P. Hofacker, Professor Walter Silz, Professor René Wellek, Professor Edwin H. Zeydel, and the members of the Committee on Publications at Washington University. Needless to say, this study of Tieck is indebted to Professor Zeydel's scholarship in a much more general sense as well. Warm thanks go also to Josephine Immerwahr for her encouragement, patience, and practical assistance.

R. M. I.

March, 1953

CONTENTS

CONTENTS

INTRODUCTION

"Truly, the humor of Tieck's fairy tales and comedies was not lacking in the most arbitrary treatment of the objective world, in the fantastic and in irony, in self-parody and in transcendence of the prosaic laws of reality. Therefore Friedrich Schlegel could quite properly make use of the Berlin poet as an illustration of his esthetic doctrine. The tomcat Hinze 'strolling about on the roof of dramatic art'[1] was well-nigh a symbol of irony."[2]

The association of Friedrich Schlegel's "Romantic irony"[3] with the fantastic comedies of Ludwig Tieck, epitomized in these words of Haym, is a time-honored tradition of German literary history. Hermann Hettner, decades before Haym, found the "maddest and most original effervescence" of Romantic irony in Tieck's dramatized fairly tales,[4] and among the most recent critics as well, one is hard put to find Friedrich Schlegel's irony discussed without illustrations drawn from *Der gestiefelte Kater*, or Tieck's fantastic farces scrutinized other than beneath the lens of Schlegel's irony. It would appear as though the only issue under dispute were the authenticity or spuriousness of the Romantic irony which they display. Only one critic, Oskar Walzel, has seriously studied these plays *as comedy*, and even he never ventured to approach them without reference to Schlegel's concept of irony.

Strangely enough, no one has cited a single utterance in which Friedrich Schlegel or his brother August Wilhelm commends, repudiates, or in any way expressly recognizes the irony attributed to *Der gestiefelte Kater, Die verkehrte Welt*, or any other of Tieck's comedies. Tieck himself explains the poetic aims underlying these comedies in other terms, and, conversely, he chooses quite different works by himself and other writers to illustrate Friedrich Schlegel's concept of irony. It is the intention of the present study to view Tieck's fantastic farces from the perspective of comedy, and to this end it will employ principles of comedy enunciated by Friedrich and August Wilhelm Schlegel, implicit in Tieck's general criticism, and explicitly applied by all three to the plays in question.

First, however, some attention should be given to the traditional association of fantastic comedy with irony as it is expressed in the arguments of representative critics. The link between the two concepts is nearly always furnished by "the destruction of illusion." Some of Friedrich Schlegel's utterances on poetic irony suggest that the poet somehow communicates to his audience a consciousness that the work is a creation of his fancy. This, say the critics, is to destroy our "illusion" that the literary work portrays objective reality. In *Der gestiefelte Kater, Die verkehrte Welt*, and elsewhere, Tieck introduces the poet, the theatrical director, and the stage machinist, the performers and the audience, directly into the action of the play, constantly calling our attention, within the play itself, to the conditions of theatrical portrayal. Thus he too destroys the "illusion" of his work. The assumption of the critics that Friedrich Schlegel had in mind such practices as we find in Tieck's comedies or that Tieck was trying to do just what Schlegel advocated has caused the destruction of illusion to be taken as the characteristic expression of Schlegel's irony and made irony the touchstone for Tieck's comic style.

Even apart from the distortion of Schlegel's utterances on irony and the failure to appreciate Tieck's esthetic objectives, which are inherent in this approach, confused and primitive notions of esthetic illusion are implied. What precisely is the illusion which Tieck destroys, and what is the illusion we wish to see upheld in a fantastic, farcical comedy? A serious critic of our own time could scarcely call for illusion in the literal sense that the reader or spectator should mistake the action portrayed for ordinary objective experience, the stage-set for an actual room. Even early in the eighteenth century we find a critic, Johann Elias Schlegel, who has advanced far beyond this childish conception of artistic portrayal.[5] Nevertheless, Tieck himself and, in an earlier period, Beaumont and Fletcher, did encounter such illusion or the demand for it in theatrical audiences, and the need to satirize this illusion was one of their reasons for violating it. Occasionally one can even find so mature a critic as Lessing suggesting this naïve viewpoint.[6] One can take the concept of illusion in a potential sense, as did Johann Elias Schlegel, or as a conscious, voluntary assumption like the "make-believe" of children, but even then the principle is not applicable to every literary category, and the most mature recipients of any form will always be the least dependent upon illusion, even in some such restricted sense. If, again, we would reduce illusion to the Aristotelian comparison of objective reality with its portrayal,[7] the validity of this principle, too, will vary greatly with different forms of art and literature. The art of fantastic comedy is one of those least concerned with comparing the objects it creates and the content of ordinary experience. A similarity can serve its purposes only when coupled with the most striking dissimilarities. If the illusion of fantastic comedy is to be the esthetic delight with which we discover the hidden truth in a bizarre distortion, we can speak of the artist's success or failure in evoking the illusion, but hardly of its deliberate "destruction."

Nevertheless, the charge that Tieck violates or destroys a kind of illusion is perfectly correct. He destroys our freedom to compare and distinguish two different aspects of reality: the total objective experience, of which the stage and actors are integral parts, and the action portrayed in the play. Our minds may dwell in either one of these worlds, and for the fullest esthetic enjoyment we must inhabit both simultaneously, but we do expect to be able to differentiate them at will. We may think of the figures on the stage—whether real or merely evoked by the printed book—as actors, as characters, or as both at once, but as characters they must mean something different to us from mere actors, and we must conceive their locale of action as something other than the stage-set. Such a very strict distinction between the world of the play and our total world to which the stage belongs has characterized Occidental drama for the past few centuries, but it is not indispensable to theatrical representation as such. The two levels of experience were not so clearly demarcated in the ancient theater, and the border line is even more obscure in medieval and Oriental drama. This "illusion" of theatrical representation was sacrosanct in serious Occidental drama in the eighteenth and nineteenth centuries, but it is not infrequently violated in our own time.

To spectators or readers who expect a clear separation between the world portrayed in the play and the world of their common experience, any confusion of the two or transgression of the one upon the other comes as a shock. This happens when the characters speak to us as actors, allude to us as spectators, to the theater, the dramatist, or the play of which they are a part. Such behavior will be the more jarring, the more rigid the differentiation to which the audience is accustomed; the shock must have been more severe for the eighteenth-century audiences of *Der gestiefelte Kater* and of Holberg's *Ulysses of Ithaca* than for the audiences of Aristophanes or of Beaumont and Fletcher. However, a confusion between the two worlds simultaneously before our eyes upon the stage will always be more jolting than the analogous state of affairs in narrative literature, as it is contrived, for example, by Laurence Sterne and Jean Paul Richter. In a serious drama, a sudden breakdown of the barrier between action and theater strikes us as grotesque, but in a farcical comedy, intended to appear nonsensical and incongruous throughout, a shock of this kind may become an effective source of laughter. If we have been put in the mood for fun, we shall find it intensely funny to hear the characters talking about the play, the theater, and ourselves. But like any other comic device, this one requires a fresh, swift, and dexterous execution; excessively repeated, prolonged, or elaborated, it falls prey to the law of diminishing returns.

If there is esthetic justification for a comic style so farcical and nonsensical that it treats nothing seriously or rationally, then it can legitimately violate the rational principle of theatrical representation. The distinction between action and theater, character and actor, will cease to be an objective per se, and a collapse of the barrier may serve comic purposes. The dramatist will not thereby destroy his own creation, for this will really be the mirth he evokes and the truth he conceals in his nonsense, rather than a second objective world. The kinds of "illusion" pertinent to his art, the esthetic impression of hilarity and the esthetic delight in the discernment of an underlying verity in outlandish caricature, will in no way be imperiled by genuine fun at the expense of theatrical portrayal. If the overriding of theatrical illusion may be understood in this sense, and if we find that it was so understood by the Schlegels and Tieck, we need only determine whether Tieck employed the device successfully from a comic standpoint. We may then, in other words, properly evaluate Tieck as a comic dramatist rather than as an exemplar of "Romantic irony."

The confusion of the portrayed with the means of portrayal, like other resources of fantastic farce, depends upon the stage for its full comic effect, upon the presentation of impossible and

incongruous situations before our very eyes. The German Romanticists were notoriously incompetent as writers for the stage
and frankly intended most of their dramatic production for
reading. Tieck's work is, on the whole, no exception to the rule,
but he did write the two fantastic comedies, *Der gestiefelte Kater*
and *Die verkehrte Welt*, with a view to theatrical production.
Even though the one has been only infrequently performed, the
other not at all, they were composed for—and about—the theater,
and, at least in the case of *Der gestiefelte Kater*, the reader in-
voluntarily projects every episode onto an imagined stage. In
this limited sense, then, we can speak of theatrical values in
Tieck's fantastic comedy, and the attention paid to individual
plays in this study will partly depend upon the extent to which
such values are present.

Another factor determining our interest will be the degree to
which each play embodies fantastic comedy in the strictest sense:
its concentration upon comic effects obtained from fantastic
situations, episodes, and characters. *Der gestiefelte Kater* is,
again, the one play by Tieck which is consistently intended to
be comical and most frequently succeeds in being so. *Die verkehrte Welt* is more fantastic, but its comedy is adulterated with
lyric and idyllic ingredients and synesthetic experiments, which
are not even comical in intent. Such extraneous elements become
much more prominent in *Prinz Zerbino*. Tieck's most ambitious
effort in dramatic form, *Kaiser Octavianus*, presents an even balance of comedy and pathos, of extravagant fantasy and realism,
but its comic characters are drawn from actual life and behave
realistically, even when they fall into fantastic situations. This
and some minor works exhibiting elements or variants of fantastic comedy will be considered only to the extent that they
supply perspective for the appraisal of *Der gestiefelte Kater* and
Die verkehrte Welt or clarify the position of fantastic comedy
in the esthetic topography of Romanticism.

Besides the irony hitherto emphasized and the comedy, which
will be our main concern here, there are other esthetic criteria
that may be applied to Tieck's comic creations. As has often been
noted, most of his fantastic comedies are also satires; in them he
obviously aims his wit against the literary standards and philosophical outlook of the moribund German Enlightenment, the
sentimental drama of Iffland and Kotzebue, the banal theatrical

taste of German audiences, and various contemporary move-
ments and institutions. All of this satire has been competently
analyzed in the critical literature,[8] but we shall consider it here
in relation to Tieck's comic purposes. Literary historians have
also frequently pointed out such specifically Romantic characteristics of Tieck's fantastic comedy as its repudiation of structural
form, its exaltation of poetic fantasy over reason and objectivity,
its delight in the bizarre and grotesque, its predilection for
sources in folk literature. The present investigation will suggest
additional criteria by which *Der gestiefelte Kater* must be evaluated before it may be taken as a full embodiment, at all events, of
German Romanticism, and in this connection some attention will
also need to be paid to another kind of comedy which the
Schlegels and Tieck expressly termed romantic.

CHAPTER ONE
Tieck's Fantastic Comedies and Friedrich Schlegel's Esthetics in Literary Criticism

We shall consider here the manner in which Tieck's fantastic-comic style has been related to the esthetic thought of Friedrich Schlegel by several representative critics of the nineteenth and twentieth centuries. The much more extensive survey of the pertinent critical literature given by Professor A. E. Lussky,[1] to which this chapter is greatly indebted, is centered upon irony and therefore does not discuss Friedrich Schlegel's conception of comedy or treat of Tieck's comedies as such, apart from his other literary creation. My own analysis of Friedrich Schlegel's pronouncements on irony will be briefly summarized at the close of this chapter and may be found in more detail in a separate study.[2]

Except for a single article by Oskar Walzel,[3] all literary criticism has concurred on the affinity of Tieck's comedies with Schlegel's irony but has been sharply divided as to whether they reflect the latter faithfully. One critical tendency, unchallenged in the nineteenth century and still strongly represented in our own time, has emphasized the "subjectivity" of Friedrich Schlegel's irony, which it has found accurately exemplified in the fantastic comedy of Teick. Other critics, since the beginning of the twentieth century, have argued for the "objectivity" of Friedrich Schlegel's irony and its gross distortion by Tieck. The foremost exponent of the first tendency is Haym. The reaction against him appears first with Marie Joachimi-Dege and is then taken up more vigorously and radically by Professor Lussky. Both critical approaches consider Tieck almost exclusively for that destruction of illusion which they take as his— authentic or spurious—version of Friedrich Schlegel's irony, but they nearly always ignore the comic function of the device with Tieck. Only Oskar Walzel has attempted to evaluate as fantastic comedy the plays in which it occurs. His numerous pertinent essays span nearly half a century, but it is only his last published utterance on irony that finally divorces Schlegel's concept from the destruction of illusion[3] and thus implicitly suggests the approach of the present study.

Although Hermann Hettner was the first important literary

historian to associate Tieck's comedy with Romantic irony and anticipated the emphasis of Haym and others on subjectivity, he displays more balance than many of the later critics. He presents a decidedly sympathetic estimate of Tieck's creation as comedy, as satire, and as Romantic fantasy, but insists at the same time that these plays are the outstanding examples of irony. His discussion of Friedrich Schlegel's irony is interpolated into a general consideration of the narrative and dramatic fairy tales of Tieck and other German Romanticists. Hettner denies the charge of Hegel that this irony was an "impudent play with the most sacred interests of life" and defines it rather as "the necessary counterpart of artistic enthusiasm, the hovering of the artist over his material, his free play with it," or "the eternal law of free form." But, Hettner goes on, this law came to be "subjectively distorted" by the Romanticists into a deliberate denial of their own creation through repeated destruction of the illusion they had evoked, and this did merit the wrath of Hegel.[4]

Since Hettner declared Tieck to be the Romantic poet "in whom that mad . . . creative caprice which mocks and destroys its own creations" is most in evidence,[5] one would expect him to pronounce the harshest judgment upon Tieck's work. Instead, one finds the incongruous assertions that "Romantic irony appears in its principal and most characteristic form" in Tieck's dramatized fairy tales and that here alone "is the basis and essence of that doctrine of Schlegel to be sought," but that such tales were at the same time the only products of German Romanticism to fulfill the requirements of art and exhibit unity of form and content. According to Hettner, the "pure form" of Tieck's comedies, liberated from the importunities of subject matter, justifies their "persiflage" of their own content. He notes that Aristophanes likewise presented a topsy-turvy world *(verkehrte Welt)* governed only by chance, caprice, and whimsy, and deliberately interrupted the illusion of objectivity in his plays; that this same fantastic comedy came to life again in Shakespeare's *Tempest* and *Midsummer Night's Dream,* in the *fiabe* of Gozzi, and in the comedies of Holberg.

> And even though one must admit that the pitiful narrowness of the modern police state has lowered Tieck's satiric comedy from the level of great historic comedy down to a tamely limited literary comedy, that Tieck is much too reflective and has become much too deliberate from the very effort not to be so . . ., a peevish berating of Tieck's fantastic comedy

does great injustice. Whoever has spent a happy hour reading *Blaubart,*
Der gestiefelte Kater, and, above all, . . . *Fortunat* with poetic feeling,
might well be inclined to reconcile himself with this fantastic dream world
and the fine artistic irony and to take hearty delight in them.[6]

The contradiction in so generous an appreciation of both
fantastic comedy and the irony that it is said to distort results
from Hettner's confusion of each with a technical stylistic device,
the destruction of illusion. The ironic "hovering of the artist
over his material," which may involve a subtle weakening of
objective illusion, would indeed be distorted by such violent destruction of this illusion as we find in *Der gestiefelte Kater* and
Die verkehrte Welt. But Tieck's intention—in Hettner's own
words a "blissfully serene cradling of fantasy in itself, delight
and joy in its own airy creations, in its whimsy overflowing with
wit"[7]—is something quite unlike Schlegel's irony, and the wanton
sacrifice of objective representation to a joyously playful fantasy
is not the kind of "hovering" that Schlegel conceived as irony.
Furthermore, Hettner stretches his concept of fantastic comedy
to the breaking point. The fantasy of Aristophanes and of *Der
gestiefelte Kater,* which everywhere aims to be ludicrous, ought
not to be identified with the serious poetic fantasy of Shakespeare's *Tempest* or with that of dramas like Tieck's *Blaubart*
and *Fortunat,* where the supernatural is presented seriously and
the incidental comic elements are drawn largely from realistic
observation.

Tieck found a much less friendly critic in Rudolf Haym. The
tendency of his fantastic comedies toward intellectual reflection,
already noted by Hettner, is in Haym's eyes a kind of poetic
sophistry, an artificial substitute for the true poetic fantasy entirely wanting in Tieck.[8] Where Haym also takes cognizance of
the stylistic relationship between Tieck and Aristophanes, it is
to emphasize the disparity between the painstaking Athenian
artist, who endows his work with universality and a fundamen-
tally serious satiric import, and the trivial German improviser,
endowed only with a certain theatrical talent, whose *Gestiefelter
Kater* becomes monotonous after the first reading. Whereas
Aristophanes satirized the public affairs of Attica, Tieck dealt
only with ephemeral literary fads, which could not take on any
universal bearing. Above all, Haym finds "foreign . . . to
Aristophanes that self-irony with which the author of *Der gestie-*

felte Kater at every moment interrupts himself and, laughing into the mirror of his own whimsy, seems only to create his work in order to destroy the creation again."[9]

No one can dispute Haym's appraisal of the relative merit and significance of Tieck's work and that of Aristophanes, but it is misleading to suggest that Aristophanes does not interrupt the dramatic action of his plays by reference to the author, the stage, and the audience. Such instances, no less drastic than those we find in Tieck, will be cited in a later chapter. However, the Athenian does not overwork this single device, and his wealth of other fantastic comic resources makes it less conspicuous.

Haym achieves a virtual identification of the jest at the expense of theatrical representation with Friedrich Schlegel's irony by way of another concept, "transcendental poetry," as it is enunciated in Schlegel's 238th *Athenäum-Fragment*.[10] However, a closer examination of Schlegel's formulation of these two principles in this and other *Fragmente,* and his illustration of them with specific poets, shows that they are not identical.[11] The essence of transcendental poetry is a concern for the "relation of the real and ideal," and the consciousness which it means to impart is of universal philosophical and esthetic problems which are expressed in the particular poetic evocation. This includes, but is not limited to, the universal poetic laws involved in the creation of the work itself. Haym most recklessly substitutes *Der gestiefelte Kater* for Schlegel's own examples of transcendental poetry—"Pindar, the lyric fragments of the Greeks, and the ancient elegy," Goethe, and above all, the *Divine Comedy*. The transcendental quality does not lie in any overt discussion by the poet of the genesis of his particular work but in his explicit and implicit reference to philosophical and poetic universals. Schlegel only indirectly associates transcendental poetry with irony, through the subtle, indirect methods which some transcendental poets select to convey their concern for the relation of the real to the ideal.[12]

Even Tieck's most sympathetic critic, Ricarda Huch, appraises the relation of his fantastic comedy to Schlegel's irony in substantial accord with Haym. For her, irony is, like the play of children, a "constant destruction and re-creation" in which the artist demonstrates his mastery over his material, his intellectual freedom and agility.[13] This interpretation leads her to assert, without documentation from Schlegel, that "the proper artistic form of irony is comedy." Friedrich Schlegel's essay in praise of Aristophanic comedy, to which she alludes here,[14] antedates his utterances on irony by three years, and in these Schlegel never attributes irony to Aristophanes; his illustrations of the new concept are drawn from predominantly serious works, in which he points out only a subtle undertone of jest.[15]

On the other hand, Ricarda Huch more than does justice to Tieck's fantastic comedies. These she characterizes as "essentially an exultant jest over the world of philistines, over the inability of people to rise above the most immediate earthly purpose. . . . The poet's own spirit, . . . like a living, flowing horn of plenty, incessantly pours out its mischievous or profound conceits."[16] Although such passages seem to credit Tieck with the very universality and true poetic fantasy denied to him by Haym, Frau Huch elsewhere soberly admits that Tieck's fairy-tale comedies fall far short of the ideal which Friedrich Schlegel saw in Aristophanes, that they are, after all, wholly intellectual products incapable of penetrating to our innermost nature.[17]

Another exponent of the subjective approach, Anna Tumarkin, argues that the free play "with images of fantasy and subjective moods" in Tieck's tales—she is not referring solely to the comedies—manifests the "clear consciousness of eternal agility, of infinitely full chaos,"[18] by which Friedrich Schlegel defines irony in the 69th *Fragment* of his "Ideen."[19] Tieck's fantastic style was taken by Schlegel and other Romantic thinkers as "confirmation of their subjectivist theory," which avowed unconditional freedom and license and refused to accept any values as absolute.[20] One may question, however, whether Schlegel's principle of irony and Tieck's comic fantasy embody precisely the same kind and degree of subjectivity, whether the philosophical and ethical relativism of irony can find a characteristic literary expression in the playful nonsense of Tieck's fantastic jest.

The relativity inherent in Schlegel's irony is again emphasized in the thoughtful interpretation by Friedrich Gundolf. Unlike most other critics, he illustrates the principle with Schlegel's own examples: Shakespeare, Cervantes, and Goethe.[21] Nevertheless, Gundolf's essay on Tieck describes the fantastic comedies as "purely ironic works,"[22] "ironic universal poems,"[23] as though they were the culmination of Schlegel's irony. To be sure,

Gundolf does not limit Romantic irony to the outright destruction of representative illusion and recognizes its presence in works like *Kaiser Octavianus* which do not utilize this device,[24] but he emphasizes the contrast of form, content, and the act of poetic creation in Tieck's comedies and sees in the poet's concern for the creative process an effort to liberate himself from the reality of his own work through the technique of Fichtean idealism. Gundolf even compares Tieck with an Archimedes who has removed the fulcrum by which he would move the earth, the belief in his own creative objective.[25] Actually, however, *Der gestiefelte Kater* contains scant reference to the process of poetic creation; its jests are concerned with the metaphysically less profound business of staging and performing. It is most unlikely that Tieck had immersed himself in Fichte when he wrote the original version of this comedy, before his contacts with Friedrich and August Wilhelm Schlegel. The analogy with Archimedes hardly seems appropriate for this boyish farce, but in any case, if Tieck was correct in declaring its objective to be the delight in wanton madness,[26] he did not willfully remove the fulcrum.

The one-sided picture of Schlegel's irony offered by such moderate subjectivist interpreters as Gundolf is balanced, and the errors of more extreme ones like Haym are corrected, by the "objective" interpretation of Marie Joachimi-Dege. She sees the central element of irony as a voluntary self-restraint by the artist, who recognizes the inevitably finite and imperfect nature of his creation,[27] accepts it, and surveys his own limited work with a "divinely urbane smile."[28] Her interpretation of Schlegel's metaphor on the "constant alternation of self-creation and self-destruction"[29] in the process of artistic creation as referring, not to the annihilation of representative illusion, but to the mutual interplay of inspired genius and conscious design, is borne out by a careful examination of the pertinent *Fragmente.*[30]

However, Frau Joachimi-Dege also takes the further, more radical step of relating Schlegel's concept of irony to the objectivity which he had extolled in the writings of his earlier classical period, such as the essay *Über das Studium der griechischen Poesie* (1795). "This objectivity," she asserts, "is now transposed into the mind of the poet. Irony is the objectivity which rests upon the poet's *infinite* individuality." And "the chief representative of Romantic irony is by no means Tieck, who treats everything ironically, . . . but *Shakespeare,* the most objective of all objective artists."[31] Whereas the true irony of Shakespeare, in Schlegel's own words, is in a "wonderful, eternal alternation" with enthusiasm,[32] the conflict between separate inspiration and consciousness in Tieck's work demonstrates his irony to be spurious.[33]

One can agree that Schlegel's concept of irony includes a kind of objectivity, the artist's self-critical detachment from his own work, but this is not the complete concealment of the creator behind the creation which he had earlier proclaimed as the objectivity of ancient Greek poetry. His repudiation of the essay *Über das Studium der griechischen Poesie* for its "lack of indispensable irony"[34] and his acknowledgment of the "frenzy of objectivity"[35] in his writings of this earlier period surely evidence a radical break in his esthetic thought. Frau Joachimi-Dege's attempt to deny it introduces a new bias in the interpretation of irony almost as serious as those which she corrects. Her point that Tieck fell short of irony because of a conflict between inspiration and critical consciousness is suggested by an utterance of Schlegel which refers only to the agonizingly serious novel *William Lovell,*[36] so that we still have no grounds for judging the fantastic comedies as expressions of irony.

More temperate versions of the "objective" interpretation of Friedrich Schlegel's irony have been presented by two American critics, Robert M. Wernaer and Walter Silz, who both have apt definitions of Schlegel's concept. According to Wernaer, it is "the joy in the possession of the powers of an infinite spirit" and "stands for clearness of vision, for presence of mind, for restraint and calm judgment."[37] Like Socrates in philosophical dialogue, the ironic poet deliberately keeps back something of what he knows but does not thereby destroy his own work. He demonstrates the ability to "dam the flow of his spirit" without shutting it off entirely.[38] In contrast with this, Tieck uses his "destructive" irony, which "appears in its most eccentric form" in *Der gestiefelte Kater,* "mainly as an end in itself" and "as a plaything." Wernaer compares Schlegel with a puppet manager who tries "to have a good play" and never stops his puppets "from mere caprice." Tieck, however, is like one who wants to show his own hand at every moment. Thus in *Der gestiefelte Kater,* "by the use of irony on the part of the manager, who is poet, actor, audience at the same time, the dramatic illusion is destroyed, and what has the semblance of reality and of serious import is set at naught."[39] One might object to this analogy that Tieck's "puppet show" was never intended to have a semblance of reality or serious import, nor does it aim at the exhibition of the manager as an end in itself. Tieck mocks the conventions of "puppetry" (figuratively speaking in *Der gestiefelte Kater* and literally in his marionette show *Hanswurst als Emigrant*) simply to amuse himself and his spectators, and when he pokes his head into the scene, it is only part of the fun. If we are amused by his pranks, the mock show is a success; if we are bored, a failure.

Professor Silz brings out more explicitly the antithesis between an original objective, and a degenerate subjective, irony. It was intended in the critical thought of Friedrich Schlegel as a mood resulting from the "recognition of the disparity between the finite and the infinite, the limited and the absolute," as a reminder "in all finite phenomena, of the infinite," as "superior self-criticism, ridicule of the inadequacy of one's own production."[40] But this ironic attitude deteriorated in the works of other Romanticists, such as Tieck, as well as in Friedrich Schlegel's own creative effort, *Lucinde;* literary criticism has derived the "current notions of 'irony' . . . , not from the pure theory of the early Romanticists, but from its distorted, not to say burlesque, application by later Romantic writers,"[41] forgetting that "Romantic irony, which in the hands of Tieck and his followers became a vehicle of obtrusive subjectivity, was, in its original meaning and intent, altogether objective . . ."[42]

Professor A. E. Lussky has developed the ideas of Marie Joachimi-Dege into the most precise and drastic formulation of objective irony. His argument centers upon the German adjective *interessant,* which Schlegel's earliest essays contrasted, as an attribute of modern literature, with the objectivity of ancient poets like Sophocles. Lussky believes that Schlegel was using the term in the sense of the Latin verb from which it is derived, to mean that the modern poet *is in* his works. The young Friedrich Schlegel found the foremost example of modern "interesting" poetry in Shakespeare, and before 1796, deemed him inferior to Sophocles. Unlike Frau Joachimi-Dege, Lussky can recognize and offer an explanation for the revolution in Schlegel's esthetic thought which took place that year: It was not, as commonly believed, against the objectivity of the Greeks, but simply in favor of Shakespeare, whom Schlegel now discovered to be "objective" and "interesting" at the same time. This synthesis of *das Objektive* and *das Interessante,* the all-pervading presence *(inter esse)* of the poet in his completely objective creation, is Lussky's conception of Romantic irony.[43] He explains the relationship by analogy with that of God and the universe.[44] The poet Shakespeare, while not revealing himself directly in his work, in some intangible fashion instills his presence into each of the objectively portrayed characters, just as God expresses Himself in all parts of His creation.[45]

Lussky contrasts Shakespeare as the one genuinely ironic poet with others, notably Goethe, Cervantes, and Tieck, who are *interessant* but not objective and therefore could not have satisfied Friedrich Schlegel. The abrupt destruction of objective illusion, which occurs so frequently with Tieck, occasionally in *Don Quixote,* and is seen by Professor Lussky in Goethe's *Wilhelm Meister* as well,[46] is a false irony.[47] Tieck's irony was not modeled after Shakespeare, but after these two novels and those of Laurence Sterne.[48] It resulted from the artist's claim to "an utterly irresponsible liberty of thought and action."[49] To Tieck, whose "ideal was first and foremost to reveal the sovereign and arbitrary power of the author directly, . . . romantic irony came to mean the actual destruction of literary objectivity by the author's speaking in his own person in his work."[50] Owing to his example, "the name 'romantic irony,' which originally stood for sheer objectivity, the objectivity of Shakespeare, in fact, came finally to be identified in the popular conception with a very subjective literary device which did not hark back to Shakespeare at all, but rather to Cervantes, Sterne, and the Goethe of *Wilhelm Meister.*"[51]

Three chapters of Professor Lussky's book are devoted to examples of this device culled from Tieck's efforts in a variety of literary categories.[52] No account is taken of the different effect of the device in stage plays and in narrative prose, in predominantly comical works and in more serious ones, but nearly all the examples are from works written by 1801, before Tieck expressed much interest in irony. The dual tragedy *Fortunat,* which Tieck himself considered his best example of irony,[53] is not mentioned. Professor Lussky concludes that "the romantic irony of *Peter Lebrecht* and of *Der gestiefelte Kater* is, after all, just a wayward and profligate descendant of its more aristocratic and refined progenitor in *Wilhelm Meister*. . . . To speak still more plainly, what is called romantic irony in such works as *Don Quixote, Tristram Shandy, Wilhelm Meister,* . . . and *Der gestiefelte Kater, is not romantic irony at all in Friedrich Schlegel's meaning of the term,* for it lacks objectivity . . ."[54]

Professor Lussky has undoubtedly rendered criticism good service by his sharp differentiation between the irony of Friedrich Schlegel and that "destruction of objectivity" practiced by Tieck, which is usually called "Romantic irony." His debatable interpretation of Schlegel's term *interessant* need not occupy us here, but to label the comic devices of *Der gestiefelte Kater* a "spurious" version of Schlegel's irony,[55] as do Professor Lussky and others emphasizing Schlegel's objectivity, would only be justifiable if Tieck himself had tried to pass them off as exemplifications of Schlegel's concept, and of that, at least, he was innocent. Lussky once concedes that "Tieck's type of romantic irony" is "very amusing" in certain episodes of *Die verkehrte Welt*.[56] Why should he not recognize that here, as in *Der gestiefelte Kater,* the theatrical device in question was intended precisely for that purpose and judge its use by the degree of amusement it affords? A comparison of Tieck's and Schlegel's irony, on the other hand, could occupy itself much more profitably with those works of Tieck which either he or Friedrich Schlegel has expressly designated as ironic in Schlegel's sense, such as *Fortunat* and *Franz Sternbalds Wanderungen*.[57]

The painstaking appraisals of Tieck's comedy in its relation to the esthetic concepts of Friedrich Schlegel which were conducted by Oskar Walzel evince some marked changes in perspective. At the very beginning Walzel thought he could see a degeneration of Schlegel's originally objective concept of irony—the detachment of the author from his work—into its opposite, an arbitrary toying by the artist with his own creation. "What on the one hand began as a maximum of objectivity, changes over at the opposite extreme into the most unbelievable excesses of subjectivism." According to the young Walzel, this deterioration of irony was exemplified not only in Tieck's fairy-tale comedies but also in the thought of Friedrich Schlegel himself, who finally accepted the latter as better embodiments of irony than the writings of Goethe.[58]

In his numerous subsequent studies, however, Walzel appears to have discarded the idea of a radical shift in Friedrich Schlegel's esthetic theory, for in these he emphasizes subjective irony exclusively in both Schlegel and Tieck. In fact, the traditional association of irony with Tieck's comic destruction of illusion finds its most drastic expression in Walzel's *Deutsche Romantik:*

> In the early Romantic circle, creations full of Romantic irony come into being before Fr. Schlegel has further developed the doctrine of irony into a tenet of his school. . . . Tieck contributes . . . examples of the Romantic theory which served excellently for the theorists but which had not been inspired by them. . . .
>
> The most manifest and obvious form of Romantic irony and the one most richly exploited by Romanticism is the destruction of dramatic illusion. Friedrich Schlegel's definitions of Romantic irony . . . did not fail to exploit this feature, when they referred to "the histrionic style of an ordinary good Italian *buffo.*" . . .
>
> *Der gestiefelte Kater* outdoes everything which had hitherto occurred on the stage in wanton destruction of theatrical illusion and in the exuberant tripping up of all the agreements which ordinarily prevail between the stage and its spectators.[59]

The allusion to the *buffo* at the end of the 42nd *Lyceum-Fragment* cited here is the only tangible evidence in all Schlegel's utterances that he may have associated irony with an outright destruction of illusion, which was indeed practiced by the clowns of the *commedia dell' arte.* Yet the same *Fragment* contains that definition of the inward spirit of irony, "the mood which surveys everything and rises infinitely above everything limited," upon which other critics have based their "objective" interpretation. As late as 1934, Walzel's attention remained fixed on the theatrical device suggested by the allusion to the Italian popular clown, and he insisted that "Romantic irony was destined from the beginning to assert itself primarily in the destruction of illusion . . ."[60] Like Haym, he buttressed his argument by reference to the *Fragmente* on transcendental and reflective poetry,[61] without taking note of the vast difference between the serious epic and lyric poetry serving Schlegel as illustrations and the farcical jests employed by Tieck or the *buffo.*

Simultaneously, however, Walzel was devoting more attention

than any other critic to Tieck's style of comedy. His article on "Schiller und die Romantik" examines Friedrich Schlegel's early essay "Vom ästhetischen Werthe der griechischen Komödie," which exalted the "pure," fantastic comedy of Aristophanes at the expense of subsequent realistic comedy.[62] Walzel shows how Schlegel's idea of a pure expression of intoxicated joy in Aristophanes resembled Schiller's association of comedy with the beautiful as distinguished from the sublime,[63] and recalls that both the Romanticists and Schiller relentlessly combated the hybrid sentimental comedies emanating from the school of Iffland and Kotzebue; Tieck, in *Der gestiefelte Kater*, was the first German Romanticist to give reality to the idea of a purely mirthful comedy.[64]

In Schlegel's defense of the Aristophanic violation of theatrical illusion, Walzel sees a foreshadowing of the later doctrine of irony: "Friedrich Schlegel's words on the interruption of illusion in Aristophanes constitute an initial attempt to open up the great and wide territory of what was later called Romantic irony."[65] However, Walzel has no support for this view other than the mention of the *buffo* in the 42nd *Lyceum-Fragment*. It is precisely this *Fragment* which Walzel reinterprets in his final article of 1938, where he repudiates the entire argument for the intimate association of Tieck's comic devices and irony. The article is not directly concerned with comedy, for its emphasis is on the fundamental relationship between the concepts of irony of Schlegel and of the younger Romantic philosopher, Solger. But having once divorced the notion of irony from the devices of Tieck's farces, Walzel would undoubtedly have approached these solely in the light of Schlegel's essay on Aristophanes.

The crucial 42nd *Lyceum-Fragment* is devoted to the spirit of Socratic irony and the possibility of recapturing it in poetry. Affirming at the outset that "philosophy is the proper home of irony," it demands Socratic irony of all nonsystematic philosophizing, and then contrasts this "sublime urbanity of the Socratic Muse" with the inferior irony of rhetoric, which resides solely in individual passages. Only poetry can rise to the all-pervading ironic spirit of philosophy:

> There are ancient and modern poetic works which throughout the whole and in every part breathe the divine breath of irony. There lives in them a really transcendental buffoonery. Within, the mood which surveys

everything and rises infinitely above everything limited, even above its own art, virtue or genius; outwardly, in their execution, the histrionic style of an ordinary good Italian *buffo*.[66]

Walzel acknowledges that the conclusion of the *Fragment* misled other critics and himself to regard the "disturbance of illusion . . . above all else as the proper manifestation of Romantic irony," confining themselves "to this single case, among other reasons, because they . . . wanted to offer their readers something really tangible." In consequence, "Romantic irony was always viewed only as a justification for the destruction of illusion, and the destruction of illusion, as the special achievement of Romantic irony." Against this misinterpretation Walzel would now invoke "first 'the irresolvable conflict of the Absolute and the limited,'[67] and then the mood which rises infinitely above everything limited."[68]

Although it is quite clear that Walzel would now shift all the emphasis in a formulation of irony from the histrionic style of the *buffo*, as an incidental, external manifestation, to the essential inward mood, he fails to explain what the references to the *buffo* and to "transcendental buffoonery" really do mean, or how Schlegel could have associated anything of the sort with the sublimely urbane Socratic style which he finds recaptured in some ancient and modern literature.[69]

A key to these problems may be found in the metaphorical style which characterizes all Friedrich Schlegel's utterances in the last few years of the eighteenth century, but particularly the *Fragmente* published in the *Lyceum* and *Athenäum*. Time and again these oracular aphorisms employ phrases which would be meaningless literally and require figurative interpretation in harmony with their context. Critics have been prone to offer interpretations with a deceiving aura of literalness which are plausible only when the metaphors in question are considered out of context. For example, the "constant alternation of self-creation and self-destruction" of naïve irony mentioned in the 51st *Athenäum-Fragment* can have no literal meaning, whether applied to the author or to his work; the interpretation that a destruction of objective illusion is involved is already quite figurative, but it is in any case proved incorrect by the remainder of this *Fragment* and others expressing the same ideas.[70] In the case of the 42nd *Lyceum-Fragment*, we should realize that poetic works *(Gedichte),* even dramatic ones, cannot have a histrionic style; here, too, no strictly literal interpretation is possible or has ever been suggested. There is merely something in the poetic style of certain ancient and modern works which reminds Schlegel of the relation of an Italian clown to his theatrical role. Schlegel does not state that this element must be the violation of representative illusion, and the device is by no means conspicuous in the literary works that he selects as illustrations of poetic irony. An alternative interpretation—in harmony with the rest of the 42nd *Lyceum-Fragment,* with all of Schlegel's other formulations of irony, and with the examples by which he illustrates it in literature—is that just as the *buffo* always *laughs* at his comic role, so the urbane, ironic author always *smiles* over the imperfect literary media in which he is forced to express his serious poetic insights.

The choice of so extravagantly paradoxical an expression as "buffoonery" to characterize a literary style imbued with that Socratic urbanity which "rises infinitely above everything limited" typifies the language in which Friedrich Schlegel, during this period, describes specific literary works, as well as that of his aphorisms. In the ironic style of *Wilhelm Meister* he sees a "silliness [*Albernheit*] developed to transparency," a "brilliant frivolity [*Leichtsinn*] and fleeting mischief [*Mutwillen*],"[71] but he warns us that even though the author appears "to take the characters and episodes so lightly and whimsically, and almost never to mention the hero without irony," we must remember that he is "most solemnly in earnest."[72] In Boccaccio's tragic epic, the *Filostrato,* Friedrich Schlegel detects "a certain graceful silliness . . . And yet the foolish business amuses us; in fact, this very ironic insignificance constitutes its special charm, as well as the inward roguishness combined with the virtuous tone of the speeches, which are magnanimous to the point of pomposity."[73] Thus *Wilhelm Meister* and the *Filostrato,* the two works which afford Schlegel his most explicit illustrations of irony, are "silly," "frivolous," "mischievous," and "roguish," even though he recognizes their essential seriousness. If he could apply terms so like "buffoonery" to these creations, neither of which ever destroys representative illusion outright, he could speak of a style analogous to that of the Italian *buffo* in serious ironic works generally, without meaning that the authors incorporate the *buffo's* farcical reference to his own role, which is but one ingredient of his histrionic style. And he could call such buffoonery "transcendental" when the author, by smilingly exaggerating the inherent limitations and contradictions of his literary medium, subtly guides our attention to universal principles of artistic creation.

CHAPTER TWO
Friedrich Schlegel's Conception of Aristophanic Comedy

Three years before his first enunciation of irony in the *Lyceum-Fragmente,* Friedrich Schlegel had devoted the essay "Vom ästhetischen Werthe der griechischen Komödie"[1] to the spirit animating the plays of Aristophanes. This he found to be, not an urbane awareness of human and poetic limitations, not an inspiration curbed by circumspect design, nor a subtle infusion of jest into earnest—the qualities which he was later to associate with poetic irony—but rather a wild Dionysian orgy of unbridled, intoxicated rapture evoked by a poet convulsed in riotous laughter. The young critic had been sated with those tearful portrayals of domestic life as found on the contemporary German stage, which was fearful of giving offense and ashamed of merriment itself, and so he was elated to discover among the ancient Greeks the closest approximation to the ideal of pure comedy.[2]

Schooled in a philosophical approach to art by his studies in Kant and Hemsterhuis,[3] the young Schlegel feels constrained to offer a metaphysical interpretation for the intoxicated merriment, the rapturous worship of joy itself, which he traces historically to the Bacchic festival. He identifies joy with beauty, life, and love, and defines it as participation in infinite being. Its antithesis, pain, signifies isolation, or separation from infinite being. The expression of joy requires complete freedom, and comedy achieves this by surmounting such obstacles as vice, folly, and error, which external reality places in the path of freedom:

> A person . . . who is governed only by his own will and makes it evident that he is subject to neither inward nor outward barriers, exemplifies complete inward and outward personal freedom. His inward freedom is made evident by his acting in happy enjoyment of himself, from pure caprice and whim alone, deliberately without reason or contrary to reasons; his outward freedom by the mischievous spirit in which he violates outward barriers, while the law magnanimously foregoes its rights.[4]

Such freedom, which was guaranteed by the sacred origin of the Old Attic Comedy, even when it turned to secular and political topics, made its flowering in Aristophanes possible. And "if anything in the works of man can be termed divine, it is the beautiful merriment and sublime freedom" expressed in his plays.[5]

But Schlegel does not find an absolute realization of his theoretical ideal even in Aristophanes. He believes that a completely beautiful comedy could only exist at a moment in the history of a civilization when the conflicting ethical and sensual sides of human nature were harmonized and, at the same time, comic art and taste were fully developed. Such a moment was never reached in the history of Attica, for its moral culture began to degenerate at a time when the taste for comedy was still coarse. Thus, as an artist, Aristophanes belongs to an early stage in cultural history; as a man, to a period of decadence. This explains two real defects of his comedies: they are artistically coarse and morally corrupt. Yet these faults are exaggerated when judged by the conventions and prejudices of an altogether different era in history. In fact, Schlegel considers these flaws of Aristophanic comedy less serious than the artificial delicacy of his own age. He distinguishes between the coarseness, even immorality, of the Old Attic Comedy and an *esthetic* immorality, of which it has no taint. For its sensual, immoral elements do not so preponderate as to destroy the artistic harmony of the whole. Moreover, without these sensual elements Aristophanes could not have made a comic impression upon his coarse public.[6] Schlegel regards the satire of Aristophanic comedy as a further defect: "The satire of Aristophanes is very often not poetic but personal and no less demagogical than is the manner in which he flatters the desires and opinions of the people."[7]

At the same time, Schlegel defends as inherent in the nature of comedy other characteristics for which the work of Aristophanes had heretofore been attacked: the frequent destruction of theatrical illusion, lack of dramatic coherence and unity, and extreme caricature. The direct allusions to the poet and audience interspersed throughout the Aristophanic comedy are justified by "the nature of comic enthusiasm."

> This violation is not awkwardness but deliberate mischief, overflowing fullness of life, and often has no bad effect at all but rather heightens the effect, for it really cannot destroy the illusion. The highest activity of life must be operative, must destroy. If it finds nothing outside of itself, it turns back to a beloved object, to itself, its own work. It then violates in order to stimulate, without destroying.[8]

It will be observed that Schlegel defends the violation of illusion in comedy as manifesting, not the ironic detachment of any great poet from his creation, but an overflowing enthusiasm and

vitality peculiar to comedy. The paradoxical assertion that the
mention by Aristophanic characters of the poet, theater, and
spectators does not destroy the illusion of these comedies, can
only mean that they have an "illusion" apart from objective
representation upon the stage: the sensation which they evoke of
rapturous joy and unbridled freedom.

Friedrich Schlegel attributes the absence of formal dramatic
unity in Aristophanic comedy to its mixture of spiritual and
sensuous elements. The sensuous, which he here associates with
"pain," would be absent from a poetic expression of absolute joy,
but receptiveness to such poetry would require a radical change
in human nature. Man as he is cannot react fully to a manifestation of joy which does not contain a certain admixture of the
sensuous in the form of pain, ugliness, or evil. Comedy utilizes
these elements in sudden contrasts to produce the ludicrous. A
purely spiritual joy would find a placid expression permitting
of dramatic unity, but the violent, restless, mixed joy of comedy
is too sensuous, intoxicating, and distracting to allow the esthetic
enjoyment of a unified form. "It creates an intoxication of life
that carries one's spirit away with it; elements of beauty which
demand too much independent activity [of the spectator] are
lost. Perfect causal connection, inner dramatic necessity and
completeness, are much too ponderous for a light, distracting
intoxication . . ."[9] As has been observed by Walzel,[10] this is the
point where the German Classical and Romantic conceptions of
pure comedy parted company. For Schiller, comedy was an expression of calm, dispassionate, rational joy and could therefore
aspire to formal perfection.[11] The irrational, Dionysian joy on
which Friedrich Schlegel based comedy was incompatible with
dramatic symmetry. On the same ground Schlegel explains the
necessity of extreme ugliness and violently ludicrous contrasts
in the intoxication of comedy, and he thus implicitly defends
Aristophanes against another of the criticisms he has mentioned,
that his caricature is too exaggerated.[12] However, the question
whether Aristophanic caricature does or should have any underlying objective validity is not touched in Schlegel's purely subjective appraisal.

As the Old Attic Comedy lost its outward freedom and inner
vitality, it gradually gave way to the essentially different New
Comedy, whose foremost exponent was Menander. Here Schlegel

recognizes a gracious style, humane characters, and elegant dialogue, but he finds the "comic energy" of the Old Comedy replaced by elements more proper to tragedy: a delicate warmth of passion and a well-ordered plot. Whether such a mixture of tragedy and comedy is esthetically justifiable, is a question Friedrich Schlegel considers outside the scope of his essay,[13] but "the nature of the comic can only be ascertained in the unmixed, pure category."[14] By this he means not that ideal expression of pure joy untainted by any "element of evil," toward which his essay vaguely aspires, but the "unsurpassable model of beautiful merriment, sublime freedom, and comic energy" which he sees in Aristophanes.[15]

Schlegel's essay is clearly no balanced critical appraisal of the Aristophanic comedies. In attempting to explain them from the abstract premise of a pure, spiritual joy, he debases to a necessary evil the sensuous and sensual imagery from which the Old Comedy derives a great part of its comic appeal. His exclusive preoccupation with the subjective state experienced by the poet and imparted to the spectators causes him to neglect the essential truth in Aristophanes' portrayal, both of individual contemporary personalities and of fundamental and timeless elements in human nature. Again, he is unfair to the satire of Aristophanes, which, far from being mere personal polemics and demagoguery, is a major part of his artistic achievement. Schlegel's abstract approach also contributes nothing to the elucidation of specific problems in the interpretation of individual comedies,[16] and it causes him to overlook the great theatrical values of the Old Comedy.

Nevertheless, Schlegel made an important esthetic discovery: the supreme value of the Aristophanic creation as comedy; and his essay marked a turning point in Aristophanic criticism for all Europe. From Aristotle down through the eighteenth century, the Old Comedy had been regarded as inferior to that of Menander, Plautus, Terence, and their modern successors. It appeared as a kind of literary anomaly, which might afford valuable lessons in rhetoric and satire but could not be justified as an esthetic whole.

In the eighteenth century especially, the predominant estimate of Aristophanes had sunk so low that, for the most part, it is summed up in the contemptuous dictum of Voltaire: "This comic poet, who is neither comical nor a poet, would not have been allowed by us to present his farces at the Saint-Laurent Fair . . ."[17] For many centuries criticism of Aristophanic comedy had been largely absorbed in the question whether or not there was any justification for the adverse portrayal of Socrates in *The Clouds*. Lessing, who showed exceptional indulgence toward Aristophanes on this count,[18] could nevertheless see in his plays "really almost nothing but satiric dialogues."[19] Wieland had but a shallow interest in Aristophanes,[20] and even Goethe, who emulated the Attic master in his own *Vögel* as well as in *Götter, Helden, und Wieland,* impresses an American scholar, Louis E. Lord, as "on the whole indifferent to Aristophanes," evincing "little real acquaintance with his comedies."[21] Schlegel was the first literary critic to realize that Aristophanic comedy belongs in a distinct literary category, governed by esthetic principles quite unlike those of the rational and relatively sedate realistic comedy. He discovered one of these principles in the evocation of intoxicated hilarity and demonstrated from it the necessity of grotesque exaggeration, farcical and fantastic incongruities, and the Aristophanic disregard for dramatic suspense and the conventions of theatrical representation. In a history of the reception of Aristophanes from ancient times to our own day, Wilhelm Süss writes:

> If we ask to whom we really owe our freer and more jovial attitude toward Aristophanes, as compared . . . not only with the preceding centuries of modern times, but even with the later Greek and Roman ancient world, . . . to obtain the final answer we must go to . . . Romanticism . . . Only with Romanticism could all the peculiarities of Aristophanic art finally count on being understood: the unbridled, exuberant intoxication, the blasting of illusion, the burlesque popular comedy, the fantastic view of animals and the magic of fairy-tale motifs. The delight of Romantic esthetics in Aristophanic comedy rests upon the most intimate essential kinship. Nothing shows this so well as the fact that the young Friedrich Schlegel . . . in 1794 wrote an essay "Vom ästhetischen Werte der griechischen Komödie," the significance of which has been all too little heeded. . . . How new the notes here sounded were, can only be estimated by one who has sampled the flood of shallow babbling and flat rationalization which had poured down on the poet [Aristophanes] in the preceding decades, even centuries.[22]

The writings of Friedrich Schlegel's first Romantic phase, which followed the period of classicism to which this essay belonged, contain just enough mention of comedy to show that he still considered Aristophanes the unparalleled master of the art.

Schlegel's most expansive utterance on the subject at this time is the 246th *Athenäum-Fragment:*

> Magic, caricature, and materiality are the means by which modern comedy can come to resemble the ancient Aristophanic inwardly, as it can outwardly through demagogical popularity, and as it has done with Gozzi sufficiently to serve as a reminder. The essence of comic art, however, always remains its enthusiastic spirit and classical form.[23]

"Magic" would here seem to connote the fantastic, irrational nature of Aristophanic comedy, "materiality," its obscene and generally sensuous tendencies. We note an important advance from the position of the early essay in Schlegel's affirmation of Aristophanic sensuality and "demagogical popularity." These are no longer defects made inevitable by unfavorable circumstances of cultural history, but rather essential, positive qualities of comedy.[24] The association of Aristophanes with Gozzi is encountered again in the 244th *Athenäum-Fragment:* "The comedies of Aristophanes are works of art which can be viewed from all sides. Gozzi's dramas have a single perspective."[25] This selection of Gozzi from among all the moderns for comparison with Aristophanes is of special interest to us here, since Gozzi probably exerted a greater influence upon Tieck's fantastic comedies than any other single precursor.[26]

The "enthusiastic spirit" mentioned in the 246th *Athenäum-Fragment* is in obvious accord with Schlegel's early essay, but we heard nothing there of "classical form." Perhaps Friedrich Schlegel has since come to see a unified form merely in the consistent mood of joy which he attributes to Aristophanic comedy, and would call this classical to distinguish it from that legion of heterogeneous forms and moods which his contemporaneous utterances designate as romantic. At all events, the purity and unity of poetic experience, which Schlegel had hitherto exalted in all classical literature and still admired in Aristophanic comedy, are now forced to contend with his new predilection for the heterogeneity found in the "romantic" creations of the Renaissance. This conflict within Friedrich Schlegel's critical thought and taste is thrown into sharp relief when we contrast the 246th *Athenäum-Fragment* with the 60th *Lyceum-Fragment:* "All classical categories in their strict purity are now ridiculous."[27]

The difficulty of reconciling Schlegel's admiration for the

"enthusiastic spirit" and "classical form" of Aristophanic comedy with his new poetic ideals of enthusiasm tempered with irony and of myriad contrasting voices and colors combined with the symmetry of a symphony or a canvas, may account for the sparseness and brevity of the remaining allusions to Aristophanes in the *Fragmente* of the *Lyceum* and *Athenäum*. Number 154 of the *Athenäum* declares: "To one who comes fresh from Aristophanes, the Olympus of comedy, romantic persiflage seems like a long spun-out thread from a weft of Athene, like a spark of heavenly fire, the best of which has disappeared in falling to the earth."[28] Two other aphorisms mention Aristophanes as the master of wit.[29] However, his name does not appear in Schlegel's pronouncements on humor,[30] or, as already noted, in the utterances on irony.

Even where comedy is directly concerned, Friedrich Schlegel's interest during the period of the *Athenäum* is no longer concentrated upon Aristophanes. We encounter on several occasions an interest in *romantic comedy*, a term which he uses for the first time early in 1798, in connection with a critical enterprise he was then projecting with August Wilhelm:

> For the Shakespeare Letters I have drawn up the following plan . . . (1) an *overture* by me; (2) a *characterization of all romantic comedies* by you . . .; (3) a *theory* of romantic comedy in general by me, with comparison of Shakespeare's lesser contemporaries, of Gozzi, the Spaniards, Guarini, etc. . . .; (4) by you, on the *tragic use of the comic* in Shakespeare. Also on the role of the comic in his historic pieces; (5) as an antistrophe to this, something theoretical by me; (6) a characterization of Shakespeare's *wit* in general by you; (7) one of *romantic wit* by me, with reference to Ariosto, Cervantes, etc. . . . You would, I believe, have to characterize [the plays] in great detail, where this seemed advisable, but still always keep in mind the form of romantic comedy, the elements that all Shakespearean comedies have in common, and those which distinguish them from the tragedies.[31]

The projected "Shakespeare Letters" did not materialize, but the concept of a romantic fusion of tragic and comic elements in a poetically idealizing comedy gradually gained ascendancy in the criticism of both Schlegels, with Calderón assuming a position at the side of Shakespeare as exemplar. In both the critical theory of the German Romantic movement and its creative experimentation — notably in Tieck's *Kaiser Octavianus* — this "romantic" comedy must be differentiated from the "pure" or fantastic comedy which the Schlegels found in Aristophanes.

Whereas August Wilhelm tried to make room for both these literary ideals in his system of poetic theory, Friedrich seems slowly and hesitantly to have turned from the Aristophanic toward the romantic ideal. His full enunciation of the latter belongs properly to the second, Catholic, phase of his Romanticism —outside the scope of this investigation—but that the transition was completed prior to his conversion may be seen from the following lines written to August Wilhelm from Paris in September, 1802:

> I wish you would heed my conviction and recognize the special justification of the *romantic*, in the drama as elsewhere. I am becoming more and more convinced that this is the only true path, even for comedy. The ancient remains flat or becomes learned and can only be significant if taken mythologically, in which case it automatically passes into the domain of *esoteric* poetry. But the wholly modern is an unworthy and sterile material even for comedy.[32]

The twice-used "even for comedy" strongly suggests that this was the last realm of literature that Friedrich Schlegel transferred to the rule of those esthetic principles which he derived from Renaissance poetry. Even though classical literature in general had for some years appeared "flat," or at best "esoteric," in his eyes, Aristophanic comedy had retained a fascination which he could not easily shake off. But he finally reached the conclusion that a choice must be made between the unified expression of joy displayed by Aristophanes and the tragicomic synthesis achieved by the "romantic" dramatists of the Renaissance—at least where a model was to be held up for the emulation of his own contemporaries. So Friedrich Schlegel at last turned his back upon Aristophanes to embrace the romantic comedy of Shakespeare and of Calderón.

CHAPTER THREE
The Dramatic Theory of August Wilhelm Schlegel

The more adroit and practical elder brother, who disseminated, popularized, and systematized the original insights of Friedrich, was striving to gain the widest possible acceptance of the Romanticists' new critical standards and to demolish the platforms of their adversaries. August Wilhelm Schlegel, therefore, cared much less for the differences between Aristophanes and Calderón than for the opportunity to exploit both in an attack upon Molière and the realistic tradition of the eighteenth century. But for such audiences as attended August Wilhelm's public lectures in Berlin and Vienna, "pure" and "romantic" comedy could take their places in a seemingly ordered scheme of poetic theory, even though they happened to be praised for nearly opposite reasons.

Recognizing this lack of consistency in the total scheme of August Wilhelm Schlegel's dramatic theory, we still cannot afford to neglect significant critical insights which may be found in some parts of it. His interpretation of Aristophanes, in particular, provides us with a clarified and balanced development of the brilliant but immature reorientation which his brother had achieved in the essay on Greek comedy. The *Fragmente* of the *Athenäum* have given us evidence that Friedrich advanced beyond the position of that early study, but the gradual shift of his interest in other directions prevented an adequate exposition of his new appraisal. However, Friedrich had ample opportunity to communicate his ideas of this period to his brother in conversation, and in view of the general dependence of August Wilhelm's esthetic thought upon that of the younger brother, we may suspect that the modified theory of Aristophanic comedy propounded by August Wilhelm also originated with Friedrich. This theory is recorded primarily in the Berlin lectures, *Vorlesungen über schöne Literatur und Kunst* (1801-4),[1] and the Vienna lectures, *Vorlesungen über dramatische Kunst und Literatur* (1808),[2] but very similar ideas had been expressed in a series of lectures *Über philosophische Kunstlehre*,[3] delivered in Jena in

1798, and in a review, written in 1800, of E.-D. de Parny's comic epic *La Guerre des dieux.*[4]

August Wilhelm develops into a fundamental dualism the distinction between the Old and New Greek Comedy which is hastily sketched at the end of Friedrich Schlegel's essay. The plays of Aristophanes and the extinct works of a few of his contemporaries and precursors are grouped into one category called the *Komödie.* A second category, the *Lustspiel,* is made to embrace not only Menander and the Latin comedy of Plautus and Terence, but in addition, all modern European comedy from the sixteenth century on. But when August Wilhelm's historical exposition comes to some modern comedies, such as the *romantische Lustspiele* of Shakespeare, Lope, and Calderón, which do not conform to his basic definition of the *Lustspiel,* this simple dualistic system really breaks down.

For the concept of an unbridled, intoxicated joy, in which Friedrich Schlegel had found the essence of Aristophanic comedy, August Wilhelm substitutes an aimless, playful jest *(Scherz),* which he contrasts with the seriousness *(Ernst)* of tragedy.[5] The *Komödie* does not merely embody pure jest in its content; its form also is, or appears to be, a product of sheer caprice, devoid of serious aim and subject to no restraint. The *Lustspiel,* on the other hand, is more or less jesting in content, but its form is the ordered, purposive dramatic plot borrowed from tragedy:

> The New Comedy, to be sure, presents the amusing in characters, contrasting situations, and combinations of these; and the more aimlessness prevails, the more comical it becomes . . .; but amidst all the jests . . ., the form of presentation itself remains serious, that is, bound in a prescribed manner to a particular purpose. In the Old Comedy, on the other hand, the form is jesting; an apparent aimlessness and caprice prevails in it; the whole work of art is a single great jest, which again comprises within itself a world of individual jests, each seeming to claim a place for itself without concern for the others.[6]

August Wilhelm uses the same principle of aimless caprice to explain the Old Comedy's rough treatment of the actual world and of rational laws. The *Komödie* dwells in its own world of jesting, capricious fantasy, which is not governed by the principles of probability and logic that control our normal experience. Its plot may be entirely impossible, inconsequent, and nonsensical; its characters, where they are not sheer creatures of drunken fantasy, are so exaggerated as to lose all resemblance to the

historical prototypes which they caricature. But the *Lustspiel,*
which inhabits the world of actual experience, must depict plausible characters and probable events, even though not in the sense
of a slavish naturalism:

> The fact that the creators of the Old Comedy mentioned living people
> and brought them upon the stage with all attendant circumstances must
> not mislead one into thinking that they therefore portrayed definite
> individuals. For, with them, such historical personalities always have
> an allegorical meaning. . . . The comic, like the tragic, poet transposes
> his characters into an ideal element; not, however, into a world governed
> by necessity, but into one in which the caprice of inventive wit rules
> unconditionally and the laws of reality are abrogated. He is therefore
> entitled to conceive the action as boldly and fantastically as possible; it
> may even be incoherent and nonsensical . . .[7]
> Since the *Lustspiel* limits the creative activity of fantasy, it must offer
> the intellect some compensation . . . in the probability of that which is
> portrayed. . . . The *Lustspiel* must be a faithful picture of contemporary
> customs . . .[8]

August Wilhelm Schlegel finds the *Komödie* free also from the
"law of dramatic portrayal," according to which the poet is supposed to disappear behind his characters and these must not
allude to the presence of spectators. The intrusion of the poet
and mention of the audience by Aristophanes in the parabasis
and elsewhere would destroy the impressions evoked by tragedy
or the *Lustspiel,* but are in accord with the mood and essential
character of the *Komödie,* where "even dramatic form is no
longer taken in complete earnest and . . . its law is momentarily
abrogated . . ." The parabasis is actually more serious than the
rest of an Aristophanic comedy, for in it the dramatist generally
gives a candid exposition of his own views, through the medium
of the Chorus. According to August Wilhelm, this brief respite
from the otherwise purely jesting mood of comedy does not impair its esthetic unity, but affords an element of variety, without
which the aimless play might eventually become monotonous to
the spectators.[9]

Showing more awareness than his brother of the serious motives underlying the work of Aristophanes—the concern for the
conduct of the Athenian state and for public affairs in general
—August Wilhelm does not conceive the *Komödie* as utterly
devoid of serious purpose. What he attributes to Aristophanic
comedy is rather an *apparent* aimlessness *(scheinbare Zweck-
losigkeit).*[10] He recognizes that each of the comedies has its own

principal satiric purpose but argues that even this is treated playfully, apart from the parabasis, and that the addition of all sorts of other comic elements, without satiric relevance, enhances an esthetic impression of aimless caprice, so that "the purpose is made into play again."[11] Here we encounter the same implicit distinction between esthetic and representative illusion that we have already met in Friedrich.[12] The impression of aimless, jesting play, which Aristophanes is thought to sustain even while seriously pursuing a satiric objective, is the only "illusion" with which he is concerned, for he has no special interest, either polemic or artistic, in upholding the representative illusion of the theater.

August Wilhelm departs from the position of his brother's essay in that he deems satire—thus sublimated in jest—essential to the *Komödie* as a poetic category rather than a mere incidental outgrowth of Aristophanes' historical environment, and considers unrestrained attacks upon public institutions and personalities to be one more necessary manifestation of comic freedom. Thus he is led to a different explanation of the disappearance of the Old Comedy: that it died, not a natural, but a violent death, in consequence of the legal decree which canceled its privileged status and forbade the representation of actual individuals by means of masks. The *Komödie* had owed its popular appeal to the jesting "idealization" of personalities and institutions familiar to the public, and once the spice of personal mockery was removed, it lost its flavor. Now that comedy could no longer risk the animosity of individuals, it could not safely satirize even general faults of the state. "The Old Comedy flourished together with Athenian freedom, and it was the same circumstances and personalities that suppressed both."[13] The *Lustspiel,* which renounced the unlimited freedom enjoyed by its predecessor, had to offer the serious dramatic form of tragedy in compensation.[14]

We find in August Wilhelm's treatment of comedy the same affirmation of its sensuous and sensual aspects that struck our attention in Friedrich's 246th *Athenäum-Fragment.* Far from conceiving these as an "original sin" of comedy (to quote Friedrich's early essay),[15] August Wilhelm considers *Sinnlichkeit* essential even to the most abstract ideal of comedy. He does not condone all the extremes of obscenity displayed by Aristophanes; like Friedrich, he explains these on the basis of local cultural conditions,[16] but he would rather see excessive sensuality in comedy than the slightest restraint upon its freedom.[17] August Wilhelm holds that the comic character is essentially an animal creature. Whereas in tragedy the sensuous man is subordinated to, and sublimated in, the spiritual, both the *Komödie* and the *Lustspiel* subordinate man's higher side, his reason and intellect, to the physical impulses. Tragedy idealizes man as a moral being; comedy idealizes him in reverse as an animal. Aristophanes' frequent reminders of the baser needs of the body, and his wanton portrayal of animal impulses bursting the fetters imposed on them by convention, are therefore indispensable.[18] In this respect, the *Komödie* and *Lustspiel* differ only in the means by which each portrays man's physical nature. The *Komödie* presents it in a fantastic context and in glaring, exaggerated contrasts with the claims of morality; the *Lustspiel* depicts it plausibly and realistically, in the context of the particular social milieu with which it is concerned.[19]

Here, as elsewhere, the comic effect of the *Komödie* is immeasurably more acute than that of its historical successor. The one evokes raucous, side-splitting laughter, the other a smile, or at most a quiet, restrained laugh. The contrasts giving rise to their respective ludicrous effects are in the first case sharp and glaring, in the second, tempered or subtle.[20] The *Komödie* links strange, unheard-of, even impossible, events with local characteristics most typical of the environment, treats in a jocular spirit of the most serious affairs of state,[21] and gives an incongruous physical reality to fanciful metaphors of language, even exploiting these, as in *The Clouds*,[22] for its titular themes.

To all of its other incongruities, the *Komödie* adds that of impossible or irrational situations taking place bodily before our eyes: "The comic poet must everywhere explain by action the unlimited caprice which justifies and motivates his transgression of existing orders. Through immediate presence, his creations take on an incomparably bolder character, and thus there arises that incomparable madness of joy and wit against which the boldest ventures of the narrator only appear sober and limited."[23] The stage, as an actual scene of fantastic happenings, takes on a special comic function lacking in realistic comedy and brings to full realization the chaotic fullness of contrast and contradiction, which is the very essence of the *Komödie*.[24]

The unbridled freedom, irrationality, coarse animality, bizarre jest, and glaring contrast of Aristophanic comedy—these all suggest a mental state akin to intoxication. August Wilhelm follows his brother in attributing this quality to the comic spirit, which he calls "the drunkenness of poetry, the Bacchanalia of jest,"[25] and he sees its antithesis in the sobriety of the *Lustspiel*, as it is exemplified by Menander, Plautus, Terence, and many of their modern disciples. Nevertheless there are a number of *Lustspiele* which he would apparently exempt from the imputation of sobriety, such as the romantic comedies of Shakespeare and Calderón and all varieties of popular farce or burlesque masque. There are other qualities of the *Lustspiel* as well which he is unable to attribute to all varieties of modern comedy, and his makeshift of breaking down the category into a number of subdivisions only renders more striking the discrepancy between some of these and the original definition which he abstracted from the New Attic Comedy:

> Since we have defined the *Lustspiel* as a mixed category, composed of comic and tragic, poetic and prosaic elements, it becomes self-evident that several subspecies may occur within the compass of this category, according to whether the one or the other component predominates. If the poet *plays in jesting whimsy* with his own inventions, a farce results; if he confines himself to the ludicrous in situations and characters, avoiding as far as possible any serious admixtures, a pure *Lustspiel*. As seriousness gains ground, . . . it passes over into didactic or sentimental drama . . .[26]

It is evident that one of these subspecies, the "pure *Lustspiel*," is a contradiction in terms, a *pure mixture*. Another, the farce, would appear to have more affinity with the *Komödie* of Aristophanes than with the *Lustspiel* of Menander, as August Wilhelm himself elsewhere confirms.

The pattern suggested above is further complicated and confused by additional subclassifications and varying definitions of each one. Among examples of the "pure *Lustspiel*," August Wilhelm distinguishes those in which the comic effect derives from plot and those in which it derives from characters.[27] This second group he divides again into plays which exploit unconscious ludicrous traits and those in which the leading characters are deliberate sources of comedy. He terms these two techniques "the comic of observation" *(das Komische der Beobachtung)* and "the comic of caprice" *(das Komische der Willkür)*.[28] The farce, which we have just met as a subheading distinct from the "pure *Lustspiel*," is now changed to a minor division of the latter by identification with the comic of caprice.[29] And Schlegel fails to account in any of his systematic classifications for the *romantische Lustspiele* of Shakespeare and Calderón.

The one particular in which August Wilhelm Schlegel's dramatic criticism is consistent is its bias against the comic tradition of France. While it would be inaccurate to say that he belittles all French comedy, he scrupulously opposes all the comic values which were most esteemed in French criticism, attacks the very comedies—notably those of Molière—for which France is most famous, and has praise for only such French comedies as are the least significant by French critical standards. Thus the high esteem in which the French held serious studies of unwitting folly (the "comic of observation") like *Le Misanthrope* is matched by a correspondingly low evaluation on August Wilhelm's part,[30] only one step above the sentimental and didactic comedies which occupy the bottom of his scale of values. Fantastic or implausible farce, which the French considered inferior, is most prized by August Wilhelm, and the second place in his favor goes to the comedy of intrigue, where he also finds a reflection of the Aristophanic spirit:

> When the characters are only lightly suggested . . .; when the plot becomes so elaborated that the motley confusion of misunderstandings and embarrassments would seemingly have to be resolved at any moment and yet the knot is always tied anew: such a composition one may well call a play of intrigue. The French art critics have made it the fashion to set the value of this variety far below the so-called character plays, perhaps because they are too much concerned with what one can retain and take home from a play. To be sure, in the end the play of intrigue dissolves itself, so to speak, into nothingness, but why should it not be permitted at times merely to indulge in meaningful play without any other purpose?[31]

The association with Aristophanic comedy suggested in the closing words becomes explicit when August Wilhelm Schlegel discusses the "comic of caprice" in deliberately ludicrous characters. These are superior intellects who look down in amusement upon the weaknesses springing from their domination by the senses and contrive to place their own baser nature in a comic light, thus taking over some of the functions of the comic poet:

There then arises the comic of caprice . . . In it stirs the spirit of the Old Comedy: the privileged fun-maker, whom almost all stages have had under different names, . . . has inherited something of the wanton enthusiasm, and thus also some of the rights, of the absolutely free ancient comic poet—certain proof that the Old Comedy . . . was not any mere peculiarity of the Greeks, but that its essential quality has a natural basis.[32]

In his historical survey of modern European drama, August Wilhelm mentions several plays to illustrate the comedy of caprice and the farce. It would seem paradoxical that he should find the closest modern approximation of the Aristophanic spirit in a product of the French theater, were it not one virtually overlooked in the history of French literature: *Le Roy de Cocagne,* by Marc-Antoine Le Grand,

. . . a colorful supernatural farce, effervescent with the fantastic wit so seldom native to France, animated by that bright jest which, though wild to the point of frenzied gaiety, moves around and over everything in a harmless legerdemain. We might call it a graceful and meaningful piece of madness, a vivid example of the manner in which the Aristophanic category . . . could be exemplified on our stage without its improprieties and personal mockery.[33]

Other modern works which August Wilhelm praises for their farcical merriment include Goethe's *Jahrmarktsfest zu Plundersweilern*[34] and *Der Triumph der Empfindsamkeit,* in which last he notes an inclination "toward the comic caprice and fantastic symbolism of Aristophanes," but of a "tame Aristophanes in elegant society and at court."[35]

The great variety of modern comedies to which August Wilhelm Schlegel applies the term *farce* have little more in common than their paucity of serious content and their rude, sharp comic effects. Some of them are fantastic; others present gross exaggerations of real life with a generous admixture of rough physical horseplay. He credits even Molière with considerable talent in this latter, realistic kind of farce (e. g., *Le Bourgeois gentilhomme*) but emphasizes his indebtedness to Latin and Italian precursors.[36] He finds the same robust physical comedy enriched by the inventions of capricious fantasy in some earlier products of the modern European theater, such as the medieval festivals of fools[37] and the German Shrovetide plays, especially those of Hans Sachs.[38] Needless to say, he is partial to the farcical folk theater, siding with the German clown Hanswurst against Gottsched, the *commedia dell' arte* and Gozzi against Goldoni.[39]

August Wilhelm's close association of farce with the "comic of caprice" may be explained by such figures of the popular theater as Hanswurst and the Italian masks, who deliberately play up their own ludicrous weaknesses. Naturally, he also displays warm attachment to the fools and other consciously ludicrous characters in Shakespeare.[40] Although he quite properly avoids designating any Shakespearean comedy as farce, he finds comedy of caprice in plays ranging all the way from *The Merry Wives of Windsor* to *Macbeth*. August Wilhelm designates Shakespeare's comedies as *Lustspiele*, yet discerns in all of them an element of poetic fantasy which transcends his original conception of that category.[41] The supreme example of the willfully ludicrous character is provided by Falstaff, "the most pleasant and amusing good-for-nothing ever portrayed," whose "tender concern for himself is without any admixture of malice toward others," who "merely does not want to be disturbed in the comfortable peace of his sensuousness, . . . is never quite serious even toward himself, and drolly disguises his way of life, his relations with others, and his sensuous philosophy."[42]

Shakespeare furnishes examples of the comedy of intrigue as well, such as *The Comedy of Errors*[43] and *The Taming of the Shrew*.[44] Another of this type, *Love's Labour Lost*, belongs among the modern *Lustspiele*, which August Wilhelm characterizes in terms applicable to the *Komödie:* "It is a wanton bit of legerdemain; in it a whole horn of plenty full of the gayest jests is poured out. . . . The sparks of wit fly in what amounts to a veritable pyrotechnic display . . ."[45]

Most of Calderón's plays, too, fall into this last category, because they resolve an intricate situation "into nothingness." As comedies of love, they outwardly resemble the Greek and Roman *Lustspiele*, but the Spanish comic characters are not the "human animals" with purely physical motivations which August Wilhelm had found in both the Old and New Attic Comedy; they are impelled by the idealistic passions of love, honor, and jealousy. The complex web which finally melts away is in this case an interplay of conflicting ideals rather than of appetites.[46] In other words, these are *romantic* comedies of intrigue.

August Wilhelm does not define romantic comedy as a distinct category, but he does point to some characteristics which differentiate it from his two original divisions of comedy. The romantic quality may take on various forms: a *poetic* fantasy which is not primarily comical (and thus differs from the boisterously ludicrous fantasy of Aristophanes), a religious or ethical concept of human nature which transcends the limitations of ordinary mundane existence, the exotic or supernatural in a more poetic than comic guise:

> Even those dramas of Calderón with modern customs, which descend farthest toward the tone of commonplace life, enthrall us with a certain fantastic spell and cannot quite be regarded as *Lustspiele* in the ordinary sense of the word. We have seen that the so-called *Lustspiele* of Shakespeare are always composed of two heterogeneous parts, the comic, which is cast in English manners, . . . and the romantic, which is transposed to some southern landscape because the native soil was not poetic enough for it. In Spain, on the other hand, the national costume of the time could still be viewed from the idealistic side.[47]

The distinguishing idealistic or "poetic" tone of romantic comedy is usually more or less serious and sometimes borders on the tragic. In fact, in nearly all the plays of Shakespeare and Calderón the comic and tragic are mixed in varying degrees. Some, like *A Winter's Tale* and *Cymbeline,* are on the boundary between comedy and tragedy, but even in the tragedies, comic characters and episodes afford a burlesque parody of the main action and its heroes. Romantic comedy, as conceived by August Wilhelm Schlegel, is therefore not an independent category so much as a vaguely demarcated area within "romantic drama," which is itself merely the dramatic manifestation of romantic poetry. In the last analysis, the essence of romantic style, what distinguishes it from ancient classicism, is its synthesis of the opposite and heterogeneous: of "art and nature, poetry and prose, earnest and jest, recollection and foreboding, spirituality and sensuousness, the earthly and the divine, life and death."[48]

August Wilhelm Schlegel is not entirely oblivious of his own inconsistency in deprecating the fusion of serious and comic elements by the realistic *Lustspiel* and middle-class drama while extolling such a union in romantic comedy and romantic drama. He argues that Shakespeare's wealth of fantasy and his contrasting and balancing of jest and earnest exclude the sentimentality and didacticism which characterize the more serious works of Molière, the middle-class drama of Diderot, and above all, the domestic dramas of Iffland and Kotzebue. Nevertheless one cannot escape the impression that his praise of both the pure

Komödie and the mixed romantic drama at the expense of French and German realistic, middle-class comedy is strongly biased by polemic considerations. One can certainly agree that Aristophanic and Renaissance dramas surpass most of the eighteenth-century comedies mentioned by August Wilhelm Schlegel in universal poetic values, yet view with suspicion his indiscriminate attack on Molière and the best of the realistic and rational comic tradition, coupled as it is with an equally indiscriminate praise of inconsequential Shrovetide farces and the crude horseplay of Hanswurst.

On closer inspection we can recognize in his argument some fundamental limitations in the esthetics of German Romanticism. August Wilhelm Schlegel acknowledges but three fundamental elements of esthetic value wherever the comic is involved: the quantity and intensity of laughter aroused, the inventiveness and freedom of fantasy, and the idealistic transcendence of earthly considerations. He does not seem to admit poetic merit in a realistic portrayal of human society and character, in dramatic suspense, in structural form—except where it becomes an expression of inventive fantasy—or in an ethics which accepts the limitations of mundane experience and behavior. Esthetic unity is emphasized or minimized by August Wilhelm to suit his polemic convenience. The only universality which he values is variety: in mood, content, and form; he virtually ignores that universality which lies in significance to human beings of all cultures and historical ages.

This restricted system of values does not merely blind August Wilhelm to some of the finest achievements in the history of comedy: it also warps his appreciation of the very comedies which he would champion, notably those of Aristophanes. Even if we grant that there is a certain esthetic merit to laughter per se—a point of view which is not confined to Romanticism—it remains obvious that something more is essential to a significant work of art than simply the evocation of intense, sustained laughter. The hilarity of farce must be enhanced by other merits to raise a play above the level of ephemeral amusement. The artistic exaltation of medieval Shrovetide plays and festivals of fools or of the buffoonery enacted by the wandering troupes of the seventeenth and eighteenth centuries is, in most instances, as absurd as would be a similar effusion on our part over the

artistic grandeur of Donald Duck. One may go a step further
and concede that the addition of rich fantasy to raucous physical
comedy can raise farce to the level of art and does so in a few
of the cases treated by August Wilhelm—or, for that matter, in
the best work of a Walt Disney—but this is still not enough to
constitute *great* art. The fantastic farce of Aristophanes is
great art—and that is probably why we usually prefer to call it
comedy; but August Wilhelm credits it only with the two merits
just mentioned plus that of a uniform mood. What makes the
work of Aristophanes great comedy rather than mere farce is
the kind of this-worldly idealism shared by Aristophanes, Shakespeare, and Molière alike, and the universal human significance
(one might say *vertical* rather than *horizontal* universality)
which is the ultimate criterion of artistic greatness. The unity
of jesting mirth with which August Wilhelm credits Aristophanes is not infrequently violated by the ardor of Aristophanic satire, descending, at least in *The Knights,* to the level
of bitterness. But the sincerity, depth, and universal import of
Aristophanes' ethics, together with the unique personal integrity,
vitality, and strength which pervade all his work, create a higher
unity. The satire which August Wilhelm would justify solely in
terms of comic freedom[49] is an expression of the poet's idealism,
as well as of other peculiarly Aristophanic qualities, and as such
it contributes vitally to the universal significance and value of
his creation.

For all the biases and defects in August Wilhelm's appraisal
of the Old Comedy, there is considerable validity in his definition
of fantastic farcical comedy as the literary category which it
most closely approximates. Indeed, some of the rules which he
sets up for this category would be even more applicable to artists
without the transcendent greatness of Aristophanes. Such comedy in general, like most Aristophanic comedies, is subjectively
animated by a prevailing spirit of hilarious, nonsensical jest—a
more valid formulation than the rapturous joy proclaimed by
Friedrich Schlegel's essay—and in its objective portrayal, which
Friedrich had ignored, it accentuates the animal side of human
nature. It further enjoys unlimited license of exaggeration and
implausibility and may violate the laws of rational sequence,
structural symmetry, dramatic suspense, and theatrical representation applicable to other categories of drama. However, the

additional thesis of both Schlegels, that such comedy is by its very nature superior to rational, realistic, symmetrical, and dramatic comedy, is untenable. If the art of Aristophanes surpasses that of Menander or Molière, the credit belongs to Aristophanes himself and not to his literary medium. While history presents an almost unbroken tradition of good realistic comedy, in the domain of fantastic comedy it has never since recorded an artistic achievement comparable to his or, indeed, more than isolated examples of any lasting significance at all.

The contribution of August Wilhelm Schlegel to the appreciation of Aristophanes was more than offset by the baneful influence upon German literature of his—again partially valid—concepts of romantic comedy and romantic drama. Many plays of Shakespeare and Calderón combine comic and tragic elements and also have qualities which can be termed romantic. However, August Wilhelm evidently held, and certainly propagated among his younger contemporaries, the opinion that aspiring dramatists in the early nineteenth century could find no better use for their talents than to imitate the seeming heterogeneity, exoticism, and narrative diffusiveness of Shakespeare along with the other-worldly idealism of Calderón. This last, as a living conviction rooted in the culture of its age, was no less legitimate esthetic material than the so differently oriented idealism of Aristophanes, but it could not be re-created by intellectuals such as the German Romanticists, attracted simply by its symbolic meaningfulness and charm. Again, the supreme genius of Shakespeare could weave the exotic, heterogeneous, epically diffuse strands of *A Winter's Tale* or *Cymbeline* into great art, even unified drama, but such ingredients, taken as part of a literary program by limited talents and dilettantes, were to result at best in sterile exercises, more usually in pitiful monstrosities.

Before leaving August Wilhelm Schlegel we must consider that concept of poetic irony which for him was chiefly an aspect of *dramatic* theory. The subtle infusion of jest into earnest, which Friedrich saw as the literary analogy to Socratic irony, August Wilhelm usually associates with the juxtaposition and balancing of comic and tragic elements, and he holds its proper sphere to be the romantic drama:

Where the strictly tragic appears, all irony, of course, ceases.[50] However, from the avowed jest of comedy up to the point where the subjection

of mortal beings to an inevitable fate demands strict seriousness, there
is a multitude of human circumstances which . . . may be regarded with
irony.[51]

The comic characters and episodes which are interwoven with
the serious threads in Shakespeare's dramas serve to express this
irony, often through parody of the heroic figures. Everywhere
they "prevent the play from becoming a business," maintain the
serenity of spirit, and ward off that "dull, lifeless seriousness"
characteristic of sentimental drama.[52] And so it is also with the
comic *gracioso* of Calderón[53] and with Gozzi's masks.[54]

For both Schlegels the synthesis of jest and earnest serves to
express an ironic philosophy of life, the poet's recognition that
our ideals are not to be realized. The consequence is not, as later
for Solger, a somber resignation, but a subtle mockery of that
which the poet holds most in earnest. Thus when August Wilhelm
observes sensual elements intruding upon the ideal of knightly
love in medieval poetry, he sees here "an infinitely charming
contradiction . . ., but at the same time the inclination toward
irony, which, instead of lapsing into depressing seriousness,
makes a subtle jest of the consciousness of the unattainable."[55]

For the most part August Wilhelm illustrates this ironic attitude with the romantic dramas of Shakespeare. In so doing, he
subjects his brother's principle to a degree of popular trivializa-
tion;[56] yet this is not so much a distortion of Friedrich Schlegel's
theory as a shift in emphasis: from an all-pervading quality of
form to specific elements in characterization and action. And so
the expression of an ironic philosophy in the *content* of literature, to which Friedrich Schlegel only pays fleeting attention,[57]
becomes paramount in August Wilhelm's interpretation of
Shakespearean irony:

> No one has portrayed as he has the subtle self-deception, the half-con-
> scious hypocrisy towards oneself, with which even noble temperaments
> disguise that intrusion of selfish motives which is almost inevitable in
> human nature. This secret irony of characterization is to be praised for
> its unfathomable penetration, but it strikes a painful blow at enthusiasm.
> This, then, is the point which one reaches when one has had the mis-
> fortune to see through humanity, and we have no alternatives left but
> the sad truth that no virtue or greatness is entirely pure and genuine,
> and the dangerous error of assuming that the ultimate is attainable.
> Here, while he arouses the most fervent emotions, in the poet himself I
> perceive a certain coldness, but it is that of a superior spirit who has
> run the gamut of human existence and outlived feeling.[58]

Paralleling this irony in Shakespeare's characterization, Schlegel finds in his plots what common parlance calls "the irony of fate": a course of events proving utterly different or directly opposite from man's plans or anticipations.[59] Sometimes Shakespeare brings out this irony in the action of his play so strikingly that we know he does not take his creation in dead earnest:

> In Shakespeare the irony applies not merely to individual characters but often to the action as a whole. Most poets . . . take sides and demand blind faith of their readers . . . When, however, the poet by some dexterous expression turns up the less brilliant reverse of the coin, he places himself in furtive agreement with the select circle of his more discerning readers or spectators. He shows them that he has foreseen their objections and conceded them in advance, that he is not himself held captive in the subject matter which he portrays but hovers freely over it and could, if he would, relentlessly destroy the beautiful, irresistibly enticing image which he himself has conjured up.[60]

It will be noted that August Wilhelm refers here to a potential rather than actual destruction, not of *Täuschung*—the term he would have used for representative illusion—but of *Schein*. Actually, he never illustrates the principle of irony with the direct intrusion of a poet into his own work. He defines poetic irony rather as "a *more or less subtly implied* admission injected into the portrayal itself of the exaggeratedly one-sided part played therein by fantasy and feeling, by which [admission] the balance is then restored."[61]

Even August Wilhelm's comment upon a play conspicuously destroying illusion, *The Knight of the Burning Pestle*, by Beaumont and Fletcher, supplies evidence that he did not identify irony with this device. Here he simply finds irony in the commonplace sense: the authors ridicule a particular viewpoint—the completely unimaginative approach to the theater—by having their characters carry it to absurd lengths.

> It is a parody of chivalrous novels . . . But the really ingenious novelty of the play consists in the combination of this irony in regard to a chimerical misuse of poetry with another, exactly opposite, irony over the inability to comprehend any poetry, particularly the dramatic form. . . . The grocer and his wife represent . . . unpoetic spectators devoid of artistic sense. With them illusion becomes a grievous error: they react to that which is portrayed as if it were real . . . On the other hand, they show themselves incapable of all *genuine illusion*, that is, *of being vividly transported into the spirit of the poetic work* . . .[62]

We note that the passage refers to two kinds of irony and two kinds of illusion without confusing irony in either sense with the kind of illusion that actually is destroyed. The representative illusion of the stage, which the spectator-characters destroy through their ignorance, is distinguished from the "genuine" or esthetic illusion, to which they are even more inaccessible. The irony consisting in ridicule of spectator-characters may be found in any satiric farce that incorporates them, but this is neither the "Romantic" irony about which literary critics have made so much ado, nor the irony of Friedrich Schlegel. On another occasion August Wilhelm mentions irony in the commonplace sense in reference to Aristophanes;[63] the context renders it clear that subtle satiric allusions to contemporary personalities rather than the Aristophanic jests on theatrical portrayal are concerned.

CHAPTER FOUR
Tieck as a Creator of Fantastic Comedy

The flexibility of literary categories, which take on new forms in every work embodying them, makes precise definition impossible. *Fantastic comedy*, for the purposes of the present study, is the kind of literary creation which the Schlegels found approximated by Aristophanes. It employs extreme ludicrous incongruities, which could not occur in actual experience, to evoke hilarious merriment; is willfully improbable, irrational, and inconsequential, presenting impossible and incredible events before our eyes upon the stage. The phrase *phantastische Komödie* is never used by Friedrich Schlegel, rarely by August Wilhelm, but we cannot dispense with the adjective without subscribing to their untenable thesis that this is the only "genuine" or "pure" comedy. No effort will be made to distinguish sharply between fantastic comedy and farce; fantastic comedy is always farcical, and farce very often fantastic. The difference lies in significance rather than in technique. The English term "farce," and even more the German *Posse,* connote something designed solely for immediate amusement, without pretense to lasting artistic values. What was intended as the crowning event of a great national festival, and has won for itself an unquestioned place in world literature, cannot be called farce, even though it is highly farcical. For the plays of Tieck, however, which neither attained nor pretended to comparable significance, "fantastic farce" and "fantastic comedy" seem equally appropriate. Strictly speaking, these terms accurately describe only two of his plays, *Der gestiefelte Kater* and *Die verkehrte Welt*, but varying elements of fantastic comedy may be found in a number of others written over the period from 1790 to 1811.

EARLY COMEDIES

Tieck's first creative effort in comedy, *Das Reh,*[1] was a fragmentary libretto for comic opera in the style of Gozzi. Since it was later recast and expanded, with similar fantastic characters and episodes, as *Das Ungeheuer und der verzauberte Wald*, it will not require separate consideration. Tieck's other youthful ventures in the comic realm are largely realistic—in the loose sense that their comic characters and situations are meant to resemble those of our actual experience—and they also tend toward conventional rational structure. For example, when Tieck adapts Ben Jonson's *Volpone* in *Herr von Fuchs* (1793),[2] he strives for a more closely integrated plot and more careful motivation than he found in the source, and tempers the implausibly monstrous traits of some characters. The original one-act comedy *Die Teegesellschaft* (1796)[3] fits into traditional comic situations and patterns of exposition and denouement such character types as the playwright could observe in the shallow, pseudosophisticated society of late eighteenth-century Berlin. These comedies foreshadow Tieck's Romantic phase in their satiric thrusts at the German Enlightenment and in the ironic skepticism displayed by the hero of *Die Teegesellschaft*, but in form and style they are rationalistic.

Tieck's Romanticism, as far as his creative activity in the dramatic form is concerned, is generally held to begin with the seriocomic drama *Der Blaubart* (1796).[4] It has quite legitimately been associated with *Der gestiefelte Kater*—the two plays were published simultaneously, share folk-tale sources in Perrault, and were warmly acclaimed in a single review by August Wilhelm Schlegel.[5] Specifically Romantic are the mood of horror built up around *Blaubart*'s central character, the ironic philosophy of life expressed by some other figures, the obvious emulation of Shakespeare in dialogue and characterization, and the juxtaposition of the comic and tragic. In these last two qualities it approaches the Schlegels' conception of romantic drama. However, *Der Blaubart* differs markedly both from the extreme, programmatic exemplification of romantic drama later furnished by Tieck in *Kaiser Octavianus* and from the fantastic comedy of *Der gestiefelte Kater* in that it has a coherent plot with considerable dramatic suspense, follows realistic principles in the portrayal of serious and comic characters alike, and employs the traditional comic situations of realistic comedy.

The one stylistic device of *Blaubart* suggesting fantastic comedy is its deliberate anachronism: Fairy-tale characters in a medieval setting refer to esthetic and psychological principles of eighteenth-century rationalism;[6] the Bluebeard's Court Adviser suggests that a defeat could be reported in the newspapers as "an advantageous diversionary movement";[7] and so on. The incongruity involved in these anachronisms is sometimes comical, but in more serious scenes it has an ironic effect. There is pronounced irony in the solipsistic skepticism of the character Simon, the attitude to which Tieck gave fullest expression in his novel *William Lovell*.

The one-act puppet play *Hanswurst als Emigrant*, which may have antedated *Blaubart*,[8] comes much closer to the style of *Der gestiefelte Kater*. To the farcical exaggeration and buffoonery inherent in the marionette theater it adds several forms of really fantastic jest, including those at the expense of theatrical representation. Tieck had become familiar with this particular comic device through *The Knight of the Burning Pestle*, the comedies of Ben Jonson, Ludvig Holberg's satiric farce *Ulysses of Ithaca*, Gozzi's *fiabe*, and Gherardi's *Théâtre italien*. *Hanswurst als Emigrant* seems especially indebted to this last collection, which abounds in bizarre anachronisms, farcical caricatures, and clowns who fall out of their roles. However, the similarity may in part result from an emulation of the parallel German tradition kept alive by wandering troupes and puppet theaters; Tieck's hero is the selfsame Hanswurst (Jack Pudding) whom Gottsched had sought to banish from the legitimate stage.[9]

This adolescent composition also anticipates the theatrical and literary satire of *Der gestiefelte Kater* with thrusts at such exponents of middle-class banality as Iffland, Kotzebue, and J. T. Hermes,[10] but at the same time it incorporates some innocuous political satire of the arrogant emigré aristocrats who had been driven to Germany by the French Revolution. As comedy, it exploits three areas of ludicrous incongruity which we shall encounter again in *Der gestiefelte Kater:* the supernatural, the irrational, and the bizarre exaggeration and crude physical horseplay which are common to all farce. The irrational appears first of all in the multiple personality of the hero. He is at once an aristocratic emigré and a simple clown, but by reminding us of his literary history in Germany[11] he takes on a third identity: *the* Hanswurst as a theatrical institution. A related irrational pluralism is involved in the destruction of theatrical illusion: in this marionette show we must conceive the figures as both human characters and wooden dolls at the same time. The characters force us to confuse these two identities by mentioning the wood, leather, and copper of which, as puppets, they are fabricated.[12] In addition, they discuss the verse in which they speak, emphasize the need of good acting, and refer to the play as a miserable puppet show.[13]

Here, as in Tieck's subsequent fantastic comedies, the supernatural manifests itself in the comic character who undergoes miraculous transformations, and in the talking animal: The form and status of the emigré's chef have progressively deteriorated along with the fortunes of his master, so that he is now only a horse, but he is still able to speak and to shine Hanswurst's shoes.[14]

In addition to such strictly fantastic elements, Tieck's comedies contain instances of gross exaggeration, bizarre incongruity, and horseplay, which are highly implausible but do not directly contradict laws of nature or logic. The farcical incongruity most conspicuously exploited in *Hanswurst als Emigrant* is the combination of pseudopoetic, bombastic verse with the crudest of earthy sentiments and imagery. One example will suffice:

> Weder Kümmel oder Schinken
> Lindert meiner Seele Schmerz.
> Denn es sieht mein thöricht Herz
> In dem blanken Kümmelglase
> Ach, nur ihre schöne Nase,
> Und Schinken mit dem Butterbrot
> Ist Sinnbild von der Wangen Roth.[15]

As a preliminary study for *Der gestiefelte Kater,* the marionette show is supplemented by another one-act play, *Ein Prolog,* which Tieck wrote in 1796.[16] In it a number of Spectators vainly wait in a theater for the curtain to rise and ponder over the meaning of this situation. Thus everything is prepared for a play within a play such as Tieck later presents in *Der gestiefelte Kater* and *Die verkehrte Welt,* but here the "play within" never materializes. Although some of the spectator-characters caricature the contemporary taste for naturalistic domestic drama and there is a certain amount of physical comedy, the main tenor of the sketch is neither satiric nor comic. It is, rather, another expression of that peculiar solipsism which characterizes so many of Tieck's works of this time, the sensation of being lost in an unreal, dream-like existence. The Spectators come to believe that they themselves constitute the play for which they are waiting, if indeed they exist at all:

> So können wir Nachbarn allewege
> Hier gar nicht im Theater sein,
> Es ist nur Lug und Trug und Schein.
>
> . . . .
>
> Wir bilden uns nämlich ein, *wir sind*,
> Und daraus folgt denn nun geschwind,
> Dass alle Dinge, die wir so erleben,
> In uns nur als Phantome schweben.[17]

This mood, which one encounters also in *Blaubart*, *William Lovell*, and the prose tale *Der blonde Eckbert*, has some relationship to the philosophic irony of Friedrich Schlegel. On the one hand we see the horrified shudder of a person whose mind, through the doubt of even its own subjective experience, is losing its last hold on reality; on the other, the urbane, delicately cynical smile of one who denies the possibility of complete knowledge, full communication, or absolute standards in human experience. It may be further argued that the irony of *Ein Prolog* is associated with the transgression against theatrical illusion which occurs when characters themselves suggest that they are part of a play. However, there is no analogy by which such an argument can be extended to *Der gestiefelte Kater* and *Die verkehrte Welt*, for they violate theatrical illusion to express, not a horrified skepticism, but playful mirth. Whatever psychological significance we may attach to the expression of two opposite moods through similar devices, the important thing from an esthetic standpoint is that they *are* opposite. In Tieck's fantastic comedies we shall find very little that resembles either the irony of Friedrich Schlegel or the pathological solipsism of *Ein Prolog*.

DER GESTIEFELTE KATER

The significant difference between *Der gestiefelte Kater* (1797)[18] and *Ein Prolog* lies, then, less in the actual rising of the curtain upon an inner play witnessed by the Spectators than in Tieck's wholehearted exploitation of this state of affairs for satire and for comedy through the ridicule of contemporary theatrical taste and the comic entanglement of the two worlds on either side of the footlights.

The satire is achieved through the audience's comment upon each scene of the inner play: the praise which it bestows upon sentimental love episodes, tirades of humanitarianism, dazzling spectacles of fire, water, and circus animals, and imagined details of histrionic naturalism;[19] the indignation to which it is aroused whenever the simple fantasy of the fairy-tale plot offends its prosaic tastes. The approval of the Spectators also underscores the satiric material which Tieck grafts onto the inner action, the tale from Perrault. Examples of the latter are: a discourse by the King and Princess—in the tone of Iffland's and Kotzebue's sentimental middle-class dramas—on the trials of marriage;[20] the interruption of the Tomcat's rabbit hunt by two figures designated He and She—the first time with an extravagantly tender courtship, the second, with outbursts of matrimonial disillusionment;[21] and the caricature, in the person of the Tomcat himself, of sentimental humanitarian tendencies in the German Enlightenment. Thus the temptation to devour a freshly caught rabbit gives rise to the following peroration:

> Fie! for shame, Hinze! Is it not the duty of a high-minded person to sacrifice himself and his desires to the happiness of his brother creatures? That's the reason why we live, and whoever cannot do that—oh, it were better for him if he had never been born!

The stormy applause with which the audience acclaims this "beautifully human state of mind" forces Hinze to repeat the passage.[22]

The inner play also ridicules the rationalistic zeal for mathematical science by having the vacuous King question his court scholar regarding the dimensions of the planetary system simply to delight himself with the sound of vast numbers.[23] Political satire is at most faintly suggested by the stupidity and acquisitive instincts of this childish monarch and the arbitrary despotism of his fantastic neighbor, the Bugbear.[24] However, any conceivable political tendency in these characterizations is neutralized by Hinze's proclamation of liberty, equality, and the rule of the Third Estate after he has devoured the Bugbear, which elicits support for the play from a Spectator with revolutionary leanings.[25] One might say that Tieck thus ridicules in advance any political interpretation of his comedy, although the absence of serious political motives ought to be sufficiently evident from the naïveté of the fairy-tale King and the outlandish proteanism of the Bugbear. Such targets as the Prussian monarchy or the Reign of Terror lay beyond the range of Tieck's harmless satire.[26]

Even his attack upon contemporary cultural and literary tendencies, though seriously motivated, leaves the impression more of playful fun than of earnest polemics, for the obvious enjoyment which Tieck derives from his own fantastic caricatures prevents us from feeling any resentment or indignation toward their prototypes. In the last analysis, Tieck's satire is but a vehicle for comedy.

The nonsense which characterizes the jest of this comedy manifests itself, as in *Hanswurst als Emigrant,* in three basic forms: the irrational, which includes the confusion of the two worlds on either side of the footlights, the supernatural, and those grotesque incongruities which result from extreme exaggeration or physical horseplay. The jests of each type are intended to be intensely, glaringly ludicrous.[27] The comic technique of *Der gestiefelte Kater* is thus related to that of popular farce and that of Aristophanic comedy. However, since its fantasy is always intended to be comical and its comedy is all either fantastic or farcical, it has little kinship with that fantastic comedy of Shakespeare which evokes a fantastic world primarily for its poetic beauty and presents comic episodes and characters which, for the most part, are not fantastic or incredible.

The extravagant exaggeration typical of farce is especially evident in the Spectators of *Der gestiefelte Kater,* whose stupidity and bad taste could scarcely be encountered in real life. As an example we may cite their comment upon a scene involving mounted soldiers:

> WIESENER. I liked the hussars particularly well; people seldom take the risk of bringing horses on the stage—and why not? They often have more sense than human beings. I would rather see a good horse than many a human being in the more modern plays.
> NEIGHBOR. The Moors in Kotzebue—a horse is after all nothing but another kind of Moor.[28] . . . I'd rather like to see a whole play with nothing but hussars. I like the cavalry so much.[29]

or one of the effusions by the Spectator named Bötticher over the trivial naturalism which he reads into Hinze's role:

> Why, I simply can't get the excellent acting of the man who plays the cat out of my head. What a study! What art! What observation! What costuming! . . . have you noticed, I wonder, that he is not one of those black cats? No, on the contrary, he is almost entirely white and has only a few black spots; that expresses his good nature excellently; moreover, the theme of the whole play, all the emotions to which it should appeal, are suggested in this very fur.[30]

The Spectators are so intent on a prosaic analysis of motivation that they attach special dramatic significance to episodes, extraneous to the inner play, which result merely from their own interference with stage activities. They pronounce a ballet of animals, inserted by the Playwright for their own pacification, "beautifully woven into the main plot,"[31] and praise a conversation inadvertently held by him and the Stage Machinist before the curtain for its motivation of the ensuing changes in sets.[32]

Similar instances of farcical exaggeration may be found within the inner play itself, but usually interwoven with its supernatural and irrational comedy. Thus the courtship of "He" and "She" combines the time-honored ludicrous contrasts of extravagant amorous sentimentality both with their subsequent marital recrimination and with the hostile utilitarianism of an unwilling witness—the talking cat.[33] The King and Princess of the fairy tale discuss love and marriage from the standpoint of the father and daughter in middle-class drama:

PRINCESS. My most gracious father, I have always believed that my heart must first feel certain emotions before my neck would bow under the yoke of marriage. For a marriage without love, they say, is truly hell upon earth.

KING. That is right, my dear daughter. Ah, indeed, indeed, . . . a hell on earth! Alas, if only I were not qualified to discuss it! . . . Your mother, my consort of blessed memory—ah, Princess, see, the tears rush to my eyes even in my old age—she was a good queen, she wore the crown with an indescribable air of majesty—but she gave me very little peace. . . . What did I suffer! No day passed without a quarrel. . . . And still my spirit sometimes yearns for you, my blessed Klothilde! My eyes smart—I am a real old fool.[34]

The same King and Princess exhibit stupidity comparable to that of the Spectators:

PRINCESS. . . . Do tell me, pray, good peasant, why do you cut down the straw like that?

KUNZ (laughing). Why, this is the harvest, Mam'selle Queen—the grain.

KING. Grain? What do you use that for, pray?

KUNZ (laughing). Bread is baked from that.

KING. Pray, daughter, for heaven's sake, bread is baked of it! Who would ever think of such tricks! Nature is something marvelous, after all.[35]

In addition to such farcical comedy deriving entirely from the spoken lines, there is some of a purely physical kind, as illustrated by the servant who is forced to run dripping wet behind the royal carriage after rescuing the Tomcat's master from his feigned drowning.[36] Comedy of physical action is enriched by contrast with the person involved, when the King climbs a tree to obtain a better view of the landscape, then scampers down again on discovering the tree to be worm-infested.[37]

The comic effect of incidents like these derives from their farcical incredibility. However, most of the episodes in *Der gestiefelte Kater* are more strictly fantastic, involving either physical impossibility or logical anomaly. Supernatural comedy is concentrated in two characters: the Tomcat and the protean Bugbear *(Popanz)*. Hinze is a talking animal who, despite manifest feline characteristics, always passes as a human. In every word and action he embodies the ludicrous contrast between the suave, self-confident man-of-the-world and the irrepressible cat. His embarrassment over this discrepancy is concealed beneath a cloak of dignity and respectability imposing enough to silence the doubts of others, and for his own satisfaction he rationalizes his eccentric instincts with arguments typical of a sterile, pseudo-intellectual sophistication. Thus he regards his appetite for nightingales as one of those fleshly weaknesses of which even the most delicate temperaments are never quite free,[38] and he justifies his antipathy to dogs by their servility and lack of "good tone."[39]

For all that, the feline in him occasionally upsets Hinze's decorum. He snarls and claws Hanswurst when the latter grasps his paw too tightly in a friendly handshake,[40] and once he scampers up a pillar in terrified flight from the wrath of the Spectators.[41] Yet, much as such peculiar behavior puzzles the other characters, none but Hinze's own master even suspects that he is a cat. Their bewilderment may be illustrated by a groom's description to the King:

> Judging by his long white beard, one should say he is an old man, and his face completely covered with hair should almost confirm one in this opinion, but then again he has such bright, youthful eyes, such a smooth, flexible back, that one cannot understand him.[42]

The fundamental contrast of human and feline qualities in the Tomcat takes on a special coloring from his addiction to foibles which Tieck associated with the German Enlightenment. Besides affecting a sentimental humanitarianism,[43] he shows himself conversant with rationalistic learning, journalism, and literature.[44] This satiric tendency, which we find somewhat

tedious today, undoubtedly enhanced Hinze's comic appeal to
Tieck's immediate circle of listeners, readers, and potential spectators: the literary sophisticates of Berlin.

Analogous contrasts between fantastic qualities associated with
a character in the fairy tale and prosaic traits familiar to modern life are exemplified by the Bugbear. He utilizes his ability
to change form at will for the oppression and fleecing of his
subjects, to whom he is known as "the Law." By transforming
himself into a rhinoceros, he intimidates a peasant into paying
a fine, whereupon he accords the following hearing to another
subject:

> OFFICIAL. With your kindest permission, I tremble and quiver in your
> honor's formidable presence.
> BUGBEAR. Oh, this is far from my most terrible form.
> OFFICIAL. I really came—about a matter—to beg you to take my part
> against my neighbor. I had also brought this purse with me—but the
> presence of Lord Law is too frightful for me.
> (BUGBEAR *suddenly changes into a mouse and sits in a corner.*)
> OFFICIAL. Why, where has the Bugbear gone?
> BUGBEAR *(in a delicate voice).* Just put the money down there on the
> table; I will sit here to avoid frightening you.[45]

A series of transformations performed for Hinze, who likewise
addresses the Bugbear with fitting deference, is concluded by the
breezy query, "Well, my friend, how's that for tricks?"[46]

Because any reader will associate them with governmental
officialdom in his own day, the despotism and venality of the
Bugbear appear incongruous in the timeless, mythical world of
the fairy tale. The ludicrous contrast in the character thus takes
on a coloring of anachronism. This characteristic resource of
fantastic comedy and farce, which we have already observed in
Hanswurst als Emigrant, is also exploited through the rationalism and literary interests of Hinze, the allusion to newspapers
and journals,[47] and the tip with which the King rewards the
peasant for agricultural information (quoted above).[48] Similarly
anachronistic are references to contemporary literature, such as
Hinze's use of a familiar hunting song of Goethe's in the pursuit
of rabbits,[49] the King's quotation of *Don Karlos,*[50] and the satiric
darts aimed at sentimental dramas of Kotzebue[51] and Gottlieb
Stephanie.[52]

An element of logical incongruity sometimes suggested in these
anachronisms is more clearly exhibited in the confusion of par-

ticular and universal in a single character. This device, already
introduced in the Hanswurst of Tieck's puppet play, is repeated
with his namesake in *Der gestiefelte Kater*.

> HINZE. From what country do you come?
> HANSWURST. Unfortunately, only Germany. My countrymen became so
> wise at one time that they finally forbade all jokes on pain of punish-
> ment; wherever I was seen, I was called such revolting names as ridicu-
> lous, indecent, bizarre—whoever laughed at me was persecuted like
> myself, and so I was compelled to go into exile.[53]

In this play, however, not merely a character but even a setting
becomes a universal literary institution. The Princess explains
the presence of worms in the tree from which her father has so
hurriedly descended[54] by its being "a scene in nature which has
not yet been idealized; imagination must first ennoble it."[55]

The logical anomaly in our having to regard an individual
character or scene as a general institution as well is essentially
the same as the identification of character and actor, action and
play, locale and stage-set, to which *Der gestiefelte Kater* owes
its notoriety. Here, too, the phenomena appearing before us have
a dual identity, and the dramatist will not let us differentiate the
two aspects in the accustomed fashion. What results is, strictly
speaking, not so much a "destroyed illusion" as a *forced confusion* of entities which ought rationally to be kept apart.

In *Der gestiefelte Kater* this particular motif has been selected
as the principal fantastic-comic theme and is developed in a
crescendo of variations. At first we are merely given notice that
there is to be a play within a play: the tale of Puss in Boots in a
framework of Spectators, Playwright, and theatrical personnel.
Instead of our customary distinction between a dramatic world
and a theater in which this is represented, we must now differentiate between each of these two spheres as objects of representation, and a third, the actual theater in which the whole might
be enacted.

Such a state of affairs, sufficiently familiar from plays like
Hamlet and *A Midsummer Night's Dream*, would not impose too
great a strain upon our rational powers if the three concentric
spheres were kept clearly apart. However, as Tieck's comedy
progresses, the two inner spheres become less and less distin-
guishable.[56] From the very start, the Playwright and his aides
have to defend the inner play against the Spectators, but soon

this interaction between the two spheres gives way to their outright *confusion;* the characters of the inner play start to take cognizance of the Spectators in the framework:

> KING. . . . But another thing; do tell me, how, living so far away, can you speak our language so fluently!
> NATHANIEL [OF MALSINKI]. Hush!
> KING. What?
> NATHANIEL. Hush! Hush!
> KING. I do not understand.
> NATHANIEL *(softly to him).* Do be quiet about it, pray, for otherwise the audience down there will surely notice that it is really very unnatural.
> KING. It doesn't matter. They clapped before and so I can afford to take a chance.
> NATHANIEL. You see, it is only for the sake of the drama that I speak your language; for otherwise, of course, the matter is incomprehensible.[57]

This is not a mere falling out of the role by actors. The King and Nathaniel can no longer tell whether they are characters or actors; the inner play and its theatrical framework are beginning to merge. A distinction between that which is represented and those who are supposed to represent is no longer possible. This distinction is the "illusion" that has been destroyed.

From here on, not merely the actors and Playwright, but the Spectators as well, trespass upon the domain of the inner play. After the fashion of their prototypes in *The Knight of the Burning Pestle,* they impose their own will upon the theatrical personnel and force the insertion of operatic stage spectacles quite unconnected with the action of *Puss in Boots.*[58] Representative illusion is not only destroyed but sometimes created inadvertently. At the beginning of Act Three, the Playwright and Stage Machinist hold a conference on the stage, unaware of the open curtain. This scene the Spectators accept as part of the play until Hanswurst, finally called upon to clarify the situation for them, utilizes the opportunity for digs at the Playwright who has given him such a poor role.[59] At another point the Playwright literally falls into the illusion that the stage-set is a real locale: "If this were only not so far away from the king's palace, I would fetch the Pacifier;[60] . . . but am I not a fool? I became quite confused—why, this is the theater here, and the Pacifier must be somewhere behind the scenes . . ."[61]

The devices thus far mentioned constitute violations of the boundary between the inner play and its theatrical frame from

either side. But in one mad scene of the Third Act this boundary
—and with it the last vestige of rationality—becomes completely
obliterated. The court scholar Leander and Hanswurst edify the
King with a learned debate on the merits of the very play in
which they and he are characters. The victor in the disputation
is to be crowned with a hat which sits atop a high pole in the
middle of the stage:

> LEANDER. The theme of my assertion is that a recently published play
> by the name of *Puss in Boots* is a good play.
> HANSWURST. That is just what I deny.
>
> . . . .
>
> LEANDER. The play, if not perfectly excellent, is still to be praised in
> several respects.
> HANSWURST. Not one respect.
> LEANDER. I assert that it displays wit.
> HANSWURST. I assert that it displays none.
>
> . . . .
>
> LEANDER. Several characters are well-sustained.
> HANSWURST. Not a single one.
> LEANDER. Then, even if I concede everything else, the audience is well
> drawn in it.
> HANSWURST. An audience never has a character.
> LEANDER. I am almost amazed at this boldness.
> HANSWURST *(to the pit)*. Isn't he a foolish fellow? Here we are, hand
> and glove with each other and agreed in our views on taste, and he wishes
> to assert, in opposition to my opinion, that at least the audience in
> *Puss in Boots* is well drawn.
> FISCHER [a spectator]. The audience? Why no audience appears in the
> play.
>
> . . . .
>
> LEANDER. I am getting confused, but still I won't yield the victory to you.

At this point the contest is abruptly, though unconsciously, decided by the arrival of Puss in Boots himself, whom the whis-
pered behest of Hanswurst sends scurrying up the pole to fetch
the prize. Hinze is dismayed to learn later that he has thus
defeated the cause of the play in which he is hero.[62]

A complete identification of the inner play and the frame of
its production is, of course, utterly irrational. But we have
learned that such absolute nonsense is proper in fantastic
comedy, as it is conceived by the Schlegels, in so far as it helps
evoke hilarious mirth. The annihilation of theatrical illusion
does not "destroy the poet's own creation"—the charge frequently leveled against *Der gestiefelte Kater*—for such a crea-

tion is intended to be no more than a fabric of jesting whimsy. The scene just cited, as the climactic point in the development of the principal comic theme of this farce, even contributes to a semblance of structural unity. It must be conceded, however, that the complexity of the situation in this scene imposes an intellectual strain detrimental to its comic effect. In this madness there is a little too much method.

Turning now to Tieck's comic characterization as such, we find but one figure whose portrayal is intended to bear some resemblance to a real human being. This is Hinze's master, Gottlieb, a sober, honest, simple youth, who willingly subordinates himself to the superior intelligence of his cat. It is only through the incongruity of this relationship that Gottlieb achieves comic significance.

None of the remaining characters is realistic in the remotest sense of the word. The Spectators are incredible caricatures of bad theatrical taste and general stupidity. The King and Princess are a little more differentiated, but no more plausible. Strictly two-dimensional, they remind us of the playing-card royalty of *Alice in Wonderland* and of the prototypes on which Tieck actually modeled them, Gozzi's masks.[63] The arbitrary imperiousness and acquisitive instincts of Tieck's King, his sole monarchical qualities, are portrayed with a childlike whimsy appropriate to the fairy tale: "My neighbor is not a good friend of mine, so to speak, and he has a fine country; all the raisins come from there; why, I should be only too glad to have it!"[64] His principal interests, however, are such harmless sensuous pleasures as dining on rabbit, and their frustration plunges him into raging despair.[65] Similar caricature in the case of the Princess and the Court Scholar takes on a more satiric coloring from their embodiment of artificial sentimentality and vacuous rationalistic learning.

Paradoxically, the one character in this comedy with a rounded individuality is its feline hero. Tieck has succeeded in endowing Hinze's incredible combination of human and animal traits with a certain plausibility. We recognize that the two sides of his personality are in a sense quite compatible; together they form a singularly appropriate medium for the satire of a self-possessed worldly opportunism thinly disguised beneath synthetic cultural ideals. The literary sensation caused by *Der gestiefelte Kater* in its own time[66] must have owed at least as much to this one fantastic characterization with significant objective validity as to the jests involving theatrical portrayal. Similar comic principles are exhibited in the Bugbear, whose capricious proteanism aptly embodies the arbitrary despot, but Tieck does not seem to have attempted to bring this figure to life.

After Hinze, the foremost comic character is Hanswurst. In addition to the incongruous duality already mentioned, he has the function of a diabolical antagonist. His ridicule of the rationalistically learned Court Scholar reminds us of those Shakespearean fools who display more sagacity than their masters,[67] but as the principal violator of theatrical illusion he is also the adversary of the Playwright. His treacherous attacks upon the play and his alleged fondness for elaborate stage props[68] enable him to win the confidence of the audience. He espouses various conflicting viewpoints expressed by other characters out of a satanic delight in making them all appear ridiculous. In short, he exemplifies the consciously, capriciously ludicrous character so warmly championed by August Wilhelm Schlegel.[69]

The Playwright himself must be included among the fantastic-comic characters, not merely for his involuntary destruction of theatrical illusion, but as a personification of the author ever trembling before his public: "When I heard your worthy stamping—nothing has ever frightened me so, I am still pale and trembling and do not myself comprehend how I have attained to the courage of thus appearing before you."[70] Neither his own pleading nor the intervention of the Pacifier and the Machinist can save the Playwright from the wrath of the Spectators, who finally drive him from the theater in a hailstorm of paper wads and spoiled fruit.[71] This Playwright is clearly no less a ridiculous caricature than the other figures in the play, and therefore cannot simply be identified with Tieck—even though he also serves as a mouthpiece for the latter's esthetic objectives: "I wanted to make an attempt to furnish amusement by means of humor, by cheerfulness and real jokes, and hope I have been successful, since our newest plays so seldom afford us an opportunity to laugh."[72] And again in the Epilogue: "I had attempted to transport all of you back to the remote sensations of your childhood, so that you might react in that spirit to the tale enacted here without taking it for anything more important than it was intended to be."[73]

Tieck's critics have almost unanimously decried the lack of dramatic interest and unity in *Der gestiefelte Kater* and have blamed these defects upon its destruction of theatrical illusion. It is certainly true that the action of the inner play, once it becomes indistinguishable from the process of theatrical representation, is left without dramatic significance. Our interest is diverted from the plot of *Puss in Boots* to the conflict between Playwright and Spectators, and the outcome of this conflict is too obvious from the start to provide dramatic suspense. As though that were not enough, we are distracted by episodes, like the romance of "He" and "She" and the literary efforts of the Princess,[74] which have no connection with either the fairy tale or the action in the theater. If, on the other hand, we judge *Der gestiefelte Kater* as fantastic comedy or farce according to the principles enunciated by the Schlegels, the absence of dramatic unity or direction appears as an inevitable expression of the prevailing comic mood. To the extent that Tieck has succeeded in sustaining this mood, his farce may be credited with esthetic unity.

Although fantastic comedy may forego dramatic structure and suspense, it can ill afford to dispense with the vivid immediacy of the theater. As A. W. Schlegel observed,[75] the full comic effect of the impossible, the irrational, and the incredible depends on their realization before our eyes; so also the comedy in fantastic caricatures rests in large measure upon their ludicrous appearance and gestures. Above all, the stage is essential to the comic shock of a destruction of representative illusion.

The actual theatrical history of *Der gestiefelte Kater* is not too impressive, with only the one unsuccessful command performance for the enthroned Romanticist, Frederick William IV, in Tieck's lifetime. However, in our own day the comedy was adapted for the Berlin *Volksbühne* in 1921 and enjoyed successful performances there, in Heidelberg, and elsewhere.[76] Tieck states unequivocally that he intended it for the stage,[77] and his lifelong passion for the theater and subsequent activity as dramaturgist in Dresden attest his awareness of theatrical needs. *Der gestiefelte Kater* does, in fact, have theatrical merit. Its comic effect derives as much from the physical appearance, demeanor, and actions of the characters as from the dialogue.[78] The coat and claws of Hinze, his agility in climbing, the King viewing the landscape from a tree, and much more of the same sort are all good theatrical farce. Even though the play has failed to win an important place in the repertory, it was written for and about the theater, and the reader cannot fail to visualize its performance on a stage.

In the last analysis, the artistic merit and justification of *Der gestiefelte Kater* depends upon its success in evoking and sustaining a mood of nonsensical hilarity and upon the truth and significance of its satire. Any answer to these questions will contain an element of personal judgment, and therefore none can be final. The impression of this observer, and of literary history whenever it has considered the play as *comedy,* is that it affords genuine amusement and incites frequent spontaneous laughter but fails to sustain its mirth throughout. The whimsical fantasy with which it plays upon the childhood world of fairy tale, the one brilliant characterization, the usually rapid pace of jest and satire, and the fresh colloquial speech (unfortunately lost in translation) are at times overclouded with the bookish dust from excessive allusions to intellectual and journalistic fashions and *belles-lettres;* the jokes at the expense of theatrical representation—really amusing at first—begin to wear thin with constant repetition and strained elaboration. But these defects of *Der gestiefelte Kater* as farcical comedy are less serious than its shortcomings as satire. Tieck's essential satiric purpose was to assert the claims of poetic fantasy against a prosaic, unimaginative rationalism. Had he concentrated upon this worthy objective and found universally valid terms for it, *Der gestiefelte Kater* might still have been a major contribution to modern European comedy. But much of Tieck's satire was wasted on ephemeral intellectual and belletristic fads, and his extreme, narrowly antirationalistic point of view could not awaken a response outside of his immediate literary circle.

DIE VERKEHRTE WELT

Tieck's second fantastic comedy[79] is at once a much bolder and a much less successful venture into the comic and satiric territories explored by the first one. Intended to develop and intensify the fantastic-comic style of *Der gestiefelte Kater,* it falls far short of its goal and at times becomes lost upon entirely extraneous paths.

Die verkehrte Welt is a combination of Tieck's own characteristic fusion of an inner play with its theatrical frame and the
most elementary of all fantastic-comic themes: the normal state
of affairs turned topsy-turvy. From beginning to end, the confusion of inner play and frame is as absolute as at the climax of
Der gestiefelte Kater. The characters are always actors at the
same time; the Spectators do not merely criticize and interfere
with the play performed for them but become an integral part
of it, some of them migrating back and forth across the Styx-like
boundary of the footlights. The companion theme of fantastic
inversion was suggested to Tieck by his reading, in 1796, of
Christian Weise's late seventeenth-century comedy on a *Verkehrte Welt;* the applicability of Weise's theme to cultural satire
against Tieck's own topsy-turvy age could not escape his notice.[80]

The synthesis of these two comic motifs afforded a potentially
unified "plot" wanting in *Der gestiefelte Kater,* for the conflict
between prosaic rationalism and poetic fantasy no longer merely
provides a frame but animates the whole nonsensical action. In
what was supposed to have been a play about Apollo, the actor
assigned the role of clown demands the part of the god and is
relieved in his own proper capacity as Scaramuccio by a Spectator. The true Apollo is thus involved in a struggle with usurpers,
who are supported by those Spectators who do not actually ascend
the stage. The party of Scaramuccio-Apollo turns the realm of
Parnassus upside down to suit its own rationalistic and utilitarian
tastes, until his rival actor-god, the true Apollo, returns from
refuge with Admetus and Alcestis to inspire a counterrevolution.
The military victory won upon the stage by the forces of poetic
fantasy is annulled by the Spectators' demand for Scaramuccio's
restoration.

The twin irrational motifs of *Die verkehrte Welt* are not super-
imposed upon the plot from outside, as with *Der gestiefelte Kater,*
but are its innermost core; likewise, they are no longer just a
vehicle for satire but in their very essence constitute a satiric
attack upon the prosaic philosophy of life. With a dogged conviction that everything must serve some economic purpose,
Scaramuccio turns the Castalian Spring into a profitable com-
mercial spa,[81] installs a brewery, taproom, and bakery on the side
of Mount Parnassus, introduces stall-feeding for Pegasus—and
does away with free passes to the theater.[82] His prosaic outlook

on literature is typified by the dry, bureaucratic prose in which he has Thalia and Melpomene sing his praises.[83] These two are themselves curious multiple personalities: actresses, ancient Muses, and (as the comic and tragic heroines of middle-class drama in the fashion of Kotzebue) institutions of the modern theater. Their sentimental love affairs in this last capacity provide a subsidiary plot.

This brilliantly conceived unity of mock plot, irrational comedy, and satire is highly ludicrous in its broad outlines but fails dismally throughout most of its execution. Scaramuccio, the Muses, and one or two other characters are mirth-provoking for a time, and a few short scenes are hilariously funny, but otherwise that tedium which was just beginning to creep into *Der gestiefelte Kater* holds unbroken sway here. Again and again promising comic devices stale with endless repetition. The most pedantic verbosity[84] takes the place of the economy of language and pace of movement which are indispensable to comedy. It is indeed difficult to understand how the lively dialogue of *Der gestiefelte Kater* and these tiresome exercises in the logic of irrationality could stem from the same author.[85] Finally, the satire of *Die verkehrte Welt*, though it has more universal bearing than that of the earlier comedy, is seldom comical; left as an end in itself, it becomes sheer polemics.

Each fantastic-comic device of *Die verkehrte Welt* has furnished a few genuinely comic episodes. The identification of action and theater affords a delightful storm—produced by the Machinist on demand of the Spectators—in which Scaramuccio-Apollo is caught unawares and drenched to the skin.[86] Still funnier is the naval battle between the fleets of two clown admirals. Intrigued at the sight of sailors drowning in the stage, Scaramuccio arranges to sink through one of the trap doors himself—after being duly assured that he will stay dry. From one of the same trap doors the Director of the theater emerges in the role of Neptune to engage the false Apollo in a controversy which sets his own superior position in the theater against Apollo's ascendancy in the mythological hierarchy.[87]

But the device so rich in mirthful nonsense in the scenes just mentioned plunges us to the depths of boredom in the long fifth scene of Act III, where a seemingly infinite regress of concentric plays within plays is elaborated.[88] Thalia and Melpomene contrive with their suitors to enact a play before Scaramuccio in which they may gently disclose their respective sentimental attachments and the intention to desert Parnassus for the joys of the hearth. But this play within the play is itself concerned with young lovers who break the news to unsympathetic parents by means of another play *within their play*. The resulting complex of *four* concentric plays (including the outer frame of theater and Spectators) is not spontaneous nonsense but a wearisome feat of mental gymnastics.

The Muses in the scene just discussed are a degenerate example of another irrational comic device favored by Tieck: the identification of individuals with literary or theatrical institutions—in this case, the heroines of sentimental middle-class drama. Another character embodies the same principle more effectively for a time. An Innkeeper, in whose hostelry some of the action takes place, views himself and his establishment solely as theatrical conventions:

> STRANGER. Good morning, Innkeeper.
> INNKEEPER. Your humble servant, my lord.—Who in the world are you to be traveling incognito and stopping off at my inn? You must still be one of the old school; a man of the old stamp, I guess, perhaps translated from the English?
> STRANGER. I am neither a lord nor traveling incognito.—Can I have lodging here for the day and night?
> INNKEEPER. My whole house is at your service.—But, seriously, don't you plan to bring unexpected happiness to some family of this vicinity? Or to marry suddenly? Or to look up a sister?
> STRANGER. No, my friend.
>
> . . . .
>
> INNKEEPER. Then you won't get much applause.[89]

But the Theatrical Innkeeper, too, ceases to amuse after a few more such appearances.

The most important addition to Tieck's stock of fantastic-comic techniques in *Die verkehrte Welt* is the titular theme borrowed from Christian Weise. This device was familiar to Aristophanes,[90] recognized as one of the elementary comic situations by the modern esthetician Bergson,[91] and claimed as a prerogative of the comic poet by August Wilhelm Schlegel.[92] Tieck's source,[93] part of the mass of material written for pedagogical purposes by the "Schoolmaster of Zittau," not only suggested this general theme but also inspired some minor episodes in

which it is specifically applied. With Weise, a rural judge pro-
nounces various decisions reversing the normal order, including
one that shepherds must submit to shearing by their sheep.[94]
Tieck has Scaramuccio appear as a judge to pronounce this
identical decision and others which are similarly topsy-turvy,
including the characteristically Tieckian variation that an author
must do the bidding of his readers.[95] Tieck also follows Weise in
placing an Epilogue at the beginning of his comedy and a Prologue at the end.   But for all this influence in comic technique,
which Tieck himself acknowledged,[96] the two plays are not written in any similar spirit; these two topsy-turvy worlds resemble
each other in nothing so much as their equal failure to amuse.

Another irrational device more conspicuous in Tieck's *Verkehrte Welt* than in *Der gestiefelte Kater* is anachronism. In
addition to the eighteenth-century reforms which Scaramuccio
introduces on ancient Parnassus, he finds others, such as fire
insurance[97] and the inevitable newspapers,[98] already on hand.

All the comic devices we have so far considered in *Die verkehrte Welt* involve logical incongruity. The supernatural and
the merely incredible are less prominent here. Talking animals
(the sheep who rebel against their shepherds and some wild
beasts tamed by a rationalistic university education)[99] appear
only incidentally. Opportunities for farcical exaggeration and
physical comedy are afforded by the romances and married life[100]
of the Muses, a caricature of Pestalozzian educational methods,[101]
and a drunken brawl in the tavern on Parnassus.[102]

The emphasis on irrationality of situation in this comedy
carries with it the deliberate elimination of individualized character portrayal. The Spectators and several other figures are
exaggerated even beyond the point of caricature into mere ab-
stractions of stupidity; some are like fleeting apparitions in a
weird dream. Their speeches are not so much instances of
ludicrous stupidity as studied experiments in the meaningless.
If we would retain the analogy of figures from playing cards,
we must now think only of abstract linear outlines. Even the
most animated characters, such as Scaramuccio and the Innkeeper, cannot compare with the tomcat Hinze and exhibit little
of the wit and comic initiative of his antagonist, Hanswurst. As
befits a *Verkehrte Welt*, the only characters who even remotely
resemble prosaic reality are the Muses. No Playwright appears

here; the cause of poetic beauty is championed by the legitimate Apollo, Admetus and Alcestis, and the shepherds. At times, however, the tone of these characters suddenly changes from that of pastoral idyll to coarse buffoonery, an incongruity which is jarring but not comical.

The struggle between the forces of utilitarian rationalism and poetic fantasy, upon which most of the episodes in *Die verkehrte Welt* focus, affords possibilities of dramatic suspense and economy, but these are left unexploited. Furthermore, *Die verkehrte Welt* fails to communicate that unifying spirit of hilarity which can justify a willfully devious and circuitous path in fantastic comedy.[103]

Tieck informs us that in writing this comedy he "had kept the stage and its equipment in view and considered production possible if one would permit a little poetic license."[104] However, there are only a few scenes, such as the storm and the naval battle, that exploit the comic potentialities of the theater. The only kind of success conceivable for a theatrical production of this comedy is envisioned by Eduard Mörike in the novel *Maler Nolten:* The comedy is performed for the sole purpose of enabling those few who could appreciate Tieck's purpose to enjoy the bewilderment of the great philistine majority in the audience. The actor Larkens is present among the latter and impersonates a pedantic schoolmaster driven virtually mad by the spectacle.[105]

A "poetic license" which could scarcely be retained in any stage production of *Die verkehrte Welt* is the accompanying "symphony" in words, inspired perhaps by Goethe's early *Concerto Dramatico* or by an oral initiation into the synesthetic theories of Friedrich Schlegel. Tieck uses the device to some degree in the characteristically Romantic endeavor to evoke musical impressions through poetry, still more to express his own philosophical views and poetic aims,[106] but certainly not for either theatrical or comic purposes. Even apart from these "musical" interludes, there are essentially serious lyric and idyllic passages —uttered, of course, by members of the poetic faction—which completely interrupt the comic mood. Tieck did not possess the rare talent of Aristophanes for *comic* lyric poetry; his introduction of serious lyric passages into a fantastic comedy deliberately violates its essential unity and does not, like the other flaws previously mentioned, result merely from a lack of comic vitality.

Nevertheless, such passages constitute only a small part of *Die verkehrte Welt;* most of the time Tieck at least tries to communicate merriment.

PRINZ ZERBINO

Tieck's third full-length comedy, *Prinz Zerbino, oder die Reise nach dem guten Geschmack,* does not even aspire toward a unifying esthetic impression. Here the term *fantastic comedy* must be understood in a different sense. The play is certainly fantastic, and a considerable part of it is intended to be comical, but fantastic jest now shares prominence with several different components: satire per se, didactic allegory, lyrical *Stimmungspoesie,* and pastoral idyll. In this play Tieck is consciously striving, not to impart a unifying mood, but to incorporate a universe of poetic experiences. In the scheme of Romantic poetics, *Prinz Zerbino* illustrates not so much comedy as the *progressive Universalpoesie* of Friedrich Schlegel's 116th *Athenäum-Fragment.*[107]

This quest for universality extends over a volume of nearly four hundred pages in Tieck's *Schriften,* and a play of such compass and diversity could hardly have been intended for the stage. It is evident that throughout most of the writing Tieck thought of it rather as a book, for where he violates representative illusion it is usually by reference not to *spectators* or a *theater,* but to *readers* or the *print shop.* Except in a few scenes, the reader fails to visualize the action upon a stage but imagines it in the hazy, exotic landscape which one associates with much German Romantic narrative.

The stylistic inconsistency of *Zerbino* may be partially explained by the lapse of time between its inception and termination. It was begun in 1796, before *Der gestiefelte Kater,* but seems to have been written mostly in 1798, after *Die verkehrte Welt,* and was not entirely in the publisher's hands until 1799.[108] It was evidently an afterthought on Tieck's part to name it a "kind of sequel" to *Der gestiefelte Kater,*[109] for only a few minor characters in *Zerbino* are drawn from that comedy. Tieck may easily have conceived the main action of *Zerbino* and begun to write it before creating *Der gestiefelte Kater,* then grafted on the notion of a sequel, and finally written the greater part after his poetic aims and style had turned in other directions.

The central theme of a journey in search of "good taste," which is undertaken to restore the rationalism of a prince afflicted with symptoms of poetic imagination, has both comic and satiric potentialities. However, in the development of this theme, as well as of the various subplots, comedy seems deliberately subordinated to an endless polemic commentary on rationalistic literature and journalism. The satiric exponents of rationalism retained from *Der gestiefelte Kater,* Hinze—now a venerable *Hofrat*—and the court scholar Leander, are duplicated in the canine journalist Stallmeister and in Zerbino's companion, Nestor. The supernatural qualities of the Bugbear and satiric deviltry of Hanswurst merge here in the sorcerer Polykomikus and also in his servant, a devil named Jeremias.

Zerbino's chief contribution to the devices of irrational comedy is a variant of the principle of dual identity: the metaphor objectified in its literal sense and developed into a more or less elaborate allegory, usually embellished by satiric puns on the names of contemporary personalities. A notable example is the Literary Mill, which pulverizes the fine, insipid meal of rationalistic, sentimental, and sensational popular literature out of more coarse-grained sources.[110] The millstream or "fountain" is the once popular novelist August Lafontaine, the miller, J. G. Müller of Itzehoe, and each journeyman is similarly identified with a popular writer, each of whom was so quickly forgotten that just one generation later, when Tieck incorporated *Zerbino* into his collected works, he had to provide a detailed key.[111] Not content with one such allegory, Tieck locates a Forge nearby, whose master insists on welding symbolical associations into all his work.[112] Even apart from these allegories there is an abundance of puns. The most ingenious one is on Nicolai's novel *Sebaldus Nothanker,* which serves as an *emergency anchor* for the foundering rationalism of Nestor.[113]

In addition to the multitude of satiric characters and episodes, a group of "poetic" figures, this time not in conflict with their "prosaic" counterparts, are woven into a separate pastoral plot; their lyrical soul-outpourings are even more prolix than the satiric passages.

Fantastic comedy other than as a mere vehicle of satire occurs only in the one long scene devoted to the violation of representative illusion and in those few scenes which display the supernatural powers of Polykomikus and Jeremias. For almost half the play Tieck refrains from tampering with the representative illusion, then does so only occasionally until near the end, when the Prince, enraged at his failure to find good taste, turns back the stage-sets to seek it again in earlier scenes.[114] After searching through the last two, he is overpowered by the Author, Reader, Compositor, and Critic. The frustration of Zerbino's outrage against *stage properties* by personalities concerned with the *book* strikingly exemplifies the confusion of Tieck's objectives.

Considerably more comic effect is derived from Polykomikus and Jeremias. These grotesquely fantastic creatures, who are even more capriciously protean than the Bugbear of *Der gestiefelte Kater,* appoint themselves champions of the unimaginative German Enlightenment. The influence of rationalistic literature temporarily impels Polykomikus to sever relations with a Satan so "extravagant, fantastic, baroque, stubborn," and utterly without taste.[115] Jeremias, himself a devil, feigns a similar conversion to sober reason in order to make fools of Polykomikus, of the dog Stallmeister and other rationalists, and of Satan himself.

The most fantastic episode ever conceived by Tieck occurs when Jeremias entertains an Enlightened audience with a series of marionette shows parodying different types of contemporary drama.[116] Jeremias feigns indignation at one of the puppet characters, the profligate son in a middle-class drama, for his refusal to reform prior to the fifth act, and throws him clear out of the theater, whereupon the puppet harangues the audience with sentimental humanitarianism and walks off.[117] This episode is too fantastic even to be imagined on a stage; though not without a kind of grotesque comic interest, it lacks the freshness of the simpler fantastic situations in *Der gestiefelte Kater.*

There is also a certain comic value to the series of scenes laid in and around the Garden of Poesy, which form the satiric climax of the play. Here Tieck emulates Gozzi by introducing a prosaic individual, the courtier Nestor, into a fantastic situation. Nestor is disgusted with the exotic talking vegetation and put out by his failure to force properly utilitarian literary standards upon the Goddess of Poesy and the shades of great ancient and modern poets (among them, Gozzi), but he then has the gratification of conversing with solid, useful furniture and nourishing dishes.[118] However, some of this satire backfires, for the all too facile lyricism and lush imagery of the "poetic" Garden is scarcely less ridiculous than Nestor's philistine sobriety. The purely lyric and

idyllic scenes of the pastoral subplot have nothing but this un-
intentional comedy to relieve their tedium—not altogether unin-
tentional, to be sure, for Tieck undoubtedly meant to cast a delicate ironic light upon these extravagantly "poetic" passages of
Zerbino, but far exceeding the author's design.

The charge of formlessness, which many critics raise indiscriminately against all of Tieck's fantastic comedies, applies to
Prinz Zerbino in a quite different sense. *Der gestiefelte Kater* and
Die verkehrte Welt at least have a single esthetic goal, the evocation of mirth through nonsense, of which Tieck never loses sight
in the one case, and only occasionally in the other; but the very
aims of *Prinz Zerbino* are confused and irreconcilable. That
Tieck eventually himself recognized this fundamental defect
may be seen from his confession to Solger: *"Die verkehrte Welt*
is more correctly, I might say, more philosophically, constructed.
Zerbino would benefit from that necessity which in the other
[comedy] sets the various spheres in motion and better unifies
caprice, madness, and coincidence. . . ."[119] But, on the other
hand, one finds a little more wit and vitality sprinkled through
the hopelessly disjointed third comedy than can be credited to
the theoretically unified second one; perhaps for this reason,
literary historians have more frequently compared *Prinz Zerbino*
with *Der gestiefelte Kater.*

ELEMENTS OF FANTASTIC COMEDY IN OTHER PLAYS

A contemporary of *Die verkehrte Welt* and *Zerbino,* the
libretto *Das Ungeheuer und der verzauberte Wald* (1798),[120]
attains a greater measure of artistic unity than either, but its
objective is quite distinct from that of Tieck's spoken fantastic
comedy. It is an operatic adaptation of the comic technique
peculiar to Gozzi: The fantastic, endowed with a certain poetic
charm, yet sufficiently extravagant to appear in a comic-ironic
light, serves as a foil to ludicrous figures derived from the everyday world.[121]

The failure of Tieck's friend S. F. Reichardt to compose a
projected score may be partially explained by the length and
complexity of the libretto, as its author himself suggests.[122]
Though refreshingly compact and fast-moving by comparison
with *Zerbino,* Tieck's operetta could hardly be sung in less than
five or six hours. Even so severe a critic of Tieck as Haym con-

cedes that the endeavor to combine music and fantastic comedy is legitimate.[123] Aristophanes himself exploited music to a considerable extent, and in modern times outstanding success has been scored in this synthesis by Gilbert and Sullivan. What prevented Tieck from fusing these two arts was, paradoxically, a special prejudice of synesthetic early German Romanticism: the absolute antithesis which it saw between the world of music and poetry and that of prosaic utilitarianism.[124] Tieck could only imagine comic opera as an expression of this antithesis, in form as well as in content, with the music confined to a group of "poetic" characters inhabiting a fanciful realm, and most of the comedy lent by unimaginative figures capable of only spoken prose. As he explains in a preface, the function of the music would be the evocation of a "twilight dream world," which the prosaic comic characters meet with stubborn incredulity. Although both these and the fanciful characters are to be highly generalized in the manner of Gozzi's masks, the comic traits of the former should be abstracted from the everyday world.[125] Tieck's very conception of the comic operetta thus eliminated the delightful experience—familiar to us in works like those of Gilbert and Sullivan—of *fantastic-comic* characters expressing themselves in *comical song*.

The plot of Tieck's libretto revolves around the conflict between a treacherous queen, in league with evil supernatural powers, and her two stepsons. She transforms the elder of these into a destructive monster, then imposes a further plague upon the land by so enchanting a forest that all who visit it lose their sanity and are transformed into birds. The younger prince, with the aid of beneficent spirits, restores his brother and disenchants the wood as well.

Since Tieck does not intend this "twilight dream world" of good and evil magic forces as his primary source of ludicrous nonsense, he does not have the world of the theater intrude upon it directly, as in his spoken fantastic comedies. However, playful references to opera and drama through some characters,[126] together with the deliberate exaggeration of the fantastic, put added strain upon the inherently frail representative illusion of opera. In this way Tieck realizes the principle, expressed in his preface, of a play "which incessantly contradicts, without destroying, itself.''[127] To the reader, such fantasy affords, not laughter, but a continuous smiling amusement.

More intense ludicrous effects are drawn from the operetta's prosaic, unimaginative characters through their refusal to believe in the supernatural phenomena which confront them, and their involvement in physical buffoonery. For example, a duel fought over the question of the Monster's existence is broken up when the Monster himself puts both combatants to flight.[128] Of course, Tieck identifies these prosaic "masks" with German Rationalism and incorporates his usual anachronistic references to journals,[129] an Academy of Natural Sciences,[130] and the general achievements of the Enlightenment.[131] Even though the satire is milder than in the spoken comedies, the resultant intellectual tone is hardly appropriate in operetta.

The ostensibly serious fairy world of the plot takes on a delicate comic tinge from the calculated extravagance of its supernatural marvels and the sentimentality of the Monster and his brother. An oracle[132] and a scene in which the enchanted birds are made tipsy by one of the mundane comic figures[133] also provide a little direct fantastic comedy, in each case with a strong admixture of plain farcical horseplay.

Although the comic masks are intended as abstract symbols of their respective vocations, they come much closer to actual human nature than the caricatures of Tieck's spoken comedies and are portrayed with a certain sympathetic warmth. Even the archrationalist, Minister Samieli, is drawn with a lighter touch than his prototypes in *Zerbino*. Other court functionaries and servants exhibit cowardice combined with bravado, unbounded conceit, habitual drunkenness, and similar time-honored foibles of realistic comedy.

Tieck's remaining comedies and comic fragments entirely forego jests at the expense of theatrical representation but retain some of his other fantastic-comic techniques. A direct imitation of Aristophanic comedy undertaken in 1801 was never completed and was published posthumously. It is entitled *Anti-Faust oder Geschichte eines dummen Teufels*[134] and features the shade of Aristophanes among its characters.

In a Prologue Mercury appears in his ancient capacity of Psychopomp, ushering fastidious rationalistic shades into a modern Hades vitiated by circulating libraries, museums, literary journals, and humanitarian sentiments. Here Aristophanes is forced to learn how his work is championed, imitated, and trivialized on earth by the satirist Johann Daniel Falk, a leader in polemics directed against Tieck and the Schlegels. Wieland has praised Falk as a reincarnation of Aristophanes, but the Attic dramatist spurns an opportunity to return to earth through such a reincarnation. "So sah ich Land;" he puns, "—doch—Wie Land!"[135] Even in Hades, Aristophanes cannot escape the baneful influence of the corruption of his satire at the hands of Falk, for it throws him into a rationalistic fit:

> Wie kraus, confuse, wie menschenfreundlich, wird's mir im ganzen Leibe,
> Wie häuslich, wie scheusslich! O, wo lass' ich nur diese Aufklärung,
> Die Duldung, die Heterodoxie, die mir unbewusst
> Muss in den Magen gefahren sein?[136]

Tieck has obviously emulated from Aristophanic comedy, particularly *The Frogs*, the satiric exploitation of deities and shades and the puns on names of contemporary personalities. The latter device, the most atrocious instance of which is quoted above, is elaborated with reference to Böttiger, a theatrical critic whom we have already found caricatured as a Spectator in *Der gestiefelte Kater*. In *Anti-Faust* he comes floating along in a *cask* (his name means *cooper*) to take over the office of Psychopomp from the god, for, as editor of Wieland's *Neuer Teutscher Merkur*, Böttiger is the *new Mercury*.[137] After driving the rationalistic shades into his cask, he sings to them in Aristophanic style:

> Der Bötticher, Bötticher, bum, bum, bum,
> Der nimmt gern auf, was noch so dumm.
>   Kommt, ihr Verzagten,
>   Angeklagten,
> Begebt euch zu mir! Und dick, dack, duck,
>   Kommt ihr in Druck;
> In Dreck, Drack, Druck, Dreck, Drack, Druck![138]

Tieck has occasionally succeeded in this Prologue—not without some help from Ben Jonson and Goethe[139]—in recapturing a little of the rough vigor and even vulgarity[140] of Aristophanes. However, the single act which follows relapses into that tedious intellectualism and verbosity which mars so much of Tieck's comic creation. An all too garrulous Satan laments the debilitating effect of modern civilization upon his realm, while the lesser devils display their enthusiasm for reason and humanitarianism

and their familiarity with products of German literature—such
as the works on *Faust* by Goethe and Klinger and Tieck's own
Zerbino[141]—which are of special concern to their profession.
Satan is particularly enraged to learn how he has been blas-
phemed in *Zerbino,* and demands vengeance.[142] A devil named
Nickel offers to possess Nicolai and inspire him to write "Kritiken
oder Antitiecken über diesen Tieck . . ., gleichsam Kriegtieck,"[143]
but this Satan deems inadequate. It is finally decided that a
romantic devil named Dümmling shall ascend to earth, revitalize
and capture its souls, and with them feed the dying flames of Hell
back to their old fury. But one wonders how Dümmling's readings
in Tieck's *Genoveva* and *Zerbino* or even in Friedrich Schlegel's
Lucinde[144] could possibly have equipped him for the conquest of
red-blooded sinners. Surely, his time would have been better
spent in the study of Aristophanes!

Most of Tieck's later ventures in comedy exhibit the tendency
toward realism already observed in *Das Ungeheuer und der
verzauberte Wald.* The tragicomic closet drama *Kaiser Octavianus* (1801-2) devotes almost all its comedy to thoroughly realistic characters in situations which are by no means predominantly fantastic and is therefore not illustrative of fantastic
comedy as understood in the present study. Its exemplification
of such German Romantic concepts as *Universalpoesie,* romantic
comedy, and irony will be considered later in connection with
Tieck's critical thought.

Tieck's new comic realism is much more closely associated with
fantastic comedy in his last two dramatizations of fairy tales:
Leben und Tod des kleinen Rotkäppchens (1800)[145] and *Leben
und Taten des kleinen Thomas, genannt Däumchen* (1811).[146]
Though nominally a tragedy, Tieck's version of *Red Ridinghood*
is largely comical in dialogue and characterization. Supernatural
comedy is presented through the talking wolf, dog, and birds,
while the human characters, from the pert, precocious heroine
down to the most incidental figures, are drawn with painstaking
naturalistic detail. The wolf and dog are humanly conceived in
the spirit of fable, without exploitation of contrasts between
human and bestial characteristics, but Tieck adds a touch of
satiric whimsy when he portrays the wolf as a violent social
rebel like the heroes of *Sturm und Drang,* and the dog as a humanitarian philistine. A literary style as attentive to homely

detail as the German and Dutch *genre* portraiture of the six-teenth century is appropriately set in doggerel modeled after Hans Sachs. In general, Tieck is striving here for the special comic effect inherent in a realistic treatment of fantastic mate-rial, and he comes at least as close to this objective in *Rotkäpp-chen* as he did to the quite different goal of *Der gestiefelte Kater*. One "performance" is recorded to the credit of *Rotkäppchen:* In 1826 Eduard Mörike staged an impromptu adaptation with home-made marionettes at the bedside of his ailing sister Luise.[147] It is evident that the young poet was especially drawn to the spon-taneous *Volkstümlichkeit* of Tieck's play, a quality which was later to characterize the much richer creations of Mörike's own humorous fantasy. In view of the marked respect and indebted-ness which Mörike felt toward Tieck,[148] we may surmise that the latter's fantastic comedies, and in particular *Rotkäppchen,* helped stimulate the comic fantasy of *Das Stuttgarter Hutzelmännlein*.

Tieck's adaptation of *Tom Thumb* falls almost as far short of his success with *Rotkäppchen* as *Die verkehrte Welt* of *Der gestiefelte Kater*, and in both instances the second attempt is frustrated by excessive verbiage and confused objectives. In *Däumchen* the realistic dramatization of a supernatural folk tale is arbitrarily welded together with satire of literary classicism and other essentially unrelated components. The historical milieu of fifteenth- or sixteenth-century Germany is exploited as cul-tural, social, and political background but acquires very little relevance either to the action of the fairy tale or to the satire. Act I all but loses sight of comedy in the naturalistic detail with which it depicts the impoverished, oppressed life of Tom Thumb's peasant family. The rest of the play exhibits other strata of the same social order—an arrogant, ruthless aristocracy and a weak royalty exhausted by military adventures—but this social por-traiture never becomes more than a gratuitous backdrop.

Tieck eliminates some of the supernatural episodes of the Tom Thumb tradition by having them related either in a spirit of apocryphal jest—to the annoyance of Tom and his parents[149]—or as events which have already taken place off stage. In the case of the one supernatural motif directly exploited as supernatural comedy, the seven-league boots, the fantastic is presented from a realistic standpoint. The dramatist pokes fun at the implausi-bility of their magic endowment by putting them to such prosaic uses as military liaison and the fifteen-minute Continental tour of a blasé English traveler (Sir Kay), and also by adding such superfluous detail as the loss of one league's capacity with each resoling.[150] Thus the irrational fantasy which was exalted in *Der gestiefelte Kater* and *Die verkehrte Welt* is now ridiculed from the standpoint of common sense.[151] However, one fantastic device which *Däumchen* shares with Tieck's earlier comedies is the anachronism implicit in historical institutions introduced into the timeless fairy tale. To this it adds such more explicit anachronisms as late medieval politics in King Arthur's court and the modern institution of pedagogy for problem children.[152]

The curtailment of supernatural and irrational comedy in *Däumchen* is also offset by an abundance of boldly implausible episodes. Most of these appear, not in the action of the original tale, but in the subplot grafted onto it for Tieck's special satiric purposes. The brunt of this satire is now turned in a quite new direction, the ideals and literary style of German classicism. Without noticeable reference to particular works, Tieck parodies what he felt to be an artificial refinement in the sentiment and language of Goethe's and Schiller's classicism. He places some hypersensitive "beautiful souls" at the mercy of a lusty, cannibalistic ogre, and has the most trivial and vulgar matters expressed in highly stylized antique verse forms. The comic appeal of such satire resides in the crude physical humiliation inflicted upon characters affecting an unnatural delicacy, and in the extreme incongruity between content and form, reminiscent of the Aristophanic parody of Euripides.[153]

The satiric episodes center around a courtier named Semmelziege, who has fled from his wife's incessant knitting, only to fall into the hands of the giant Leidgast. This hungry ogre keeps him turning the spit over his fire or bounces him off a springboard—to amuse himself and to provide Tieck with an objectified metaphor on flights of fancy.[154] During brief respites Semmelziege consoles himself with the society of Leidgast's wife, another refined soul, who suffers unspeakable inner anguish from the brutality of her husband and sons. All these matters are presented in blank verse and trimeter replete with mythological allusions. Semmelziege's account of a particularly inopportune occasion for his wife's knitting may serve as an example:

> Einst, als des Thorus heilig Lager uns umfing,
> Am Himmel glanzvoll prangte Lunas keuscher Schein,
> Der goldnen Aphrodite Gab' erwünschend mir
> Von silberweissen Armen ich umflochten lag,
> Schon denkend, welch ein Wunderkind so holder Nacht,
> Welch Vaterlandserretter, kraftgepanzert, soll
> Dem zarten Leib entspriessen nach der Horen Tanz,
> Fühl ich am Rücken hinter mir gar sanften Schlag:
> Da wähn' ich Liebsgekose neckt die Schulter mir,
> Und lächle fromm die süsse Braut und sinnig an:
> Bald naht mir der Enttäuschung grauser Höllenschmerz,
> Das Strickzeug tanzt auf meinem Rücken thätig fort,
> Ja stand das Werk just in der Ferse Beugung, wo
> Der Kundigste, ob vielem Zählen, selber pfuscht.[155]

In all of Tieck's fantastic comedies, this is the sole jest from the domain of sexual behavior, which had been so fruitfully exploited by Aristophanes. However, the lusty appetites of Leidgast afford abundant examples of another aspect of human animality:

> I sometimes think—give me the other joint now; that's a confoundedly small lamb—I sometimes think (you know, I like to think) that one would surely find a different and better flavor . . . in eating up a good friend or a sweetheart, especially in the time of first love, when one is still not so bold and hesitates to draw near, when our whole being quivers with longing.—Give me the other bumper of wine.—Semmelziege, what do you think about that?[156]

Däumchen nowhere exploits theatrical representation itself as a source of comedy, even by the indirect methods of *Das Ungeheuer und der verzauberte Wald*. The emphasis on literary parody and the employment of verses too complex to be intelligible on a single hearing strongly suggest that *Däumchen* was intended as a closet drama. Tieck himself indicates as much in a preface, where he implicitly differentiates it from his two *Fortunat* dramas, which were written later and with the stage "again clearly in view."[157] The comic effects of *Däumchen* would be weakened rather than enhanced by theatrical presentation, and we need not regret the inability of Karl Immermann to carry out the staging he had projected in Düsseldorf.[158]

Unlike Tieck's earlier fantastic comedies, this last one carries both its plot and subplot to meaningful conclusions and is not intended to exhibit any irrationality of structure. However, the tale of Tom Thumb and its Arthurian setting are out of tune with the grotesque parody and farce of the Semmelziege episodes. Only a few years after he wrote *Däumchen*, Tieck conceded to Solger that it suffered from "too much symmetry and too little harmony" and lacked "a light, gay vitality."[159] Only the first of these three strictures would seem open to question.

TIECK, THE SCHLEGELS, AND ARISTOPHANES

Among the several examples of fantastic comedy which we have encountered in Tieck, just two, *Der gestiefelte Kater* and *Die verkehrte Welt*, approximate in their artistic purpose the "pure" comedy conceived by the Schlegels. Their essential concern is the expression of the poet's mood rather than a portrayal of objective experience. This mood, not quite the rapturous joy attributed to Aristophanes in Friedrich Schlegel's essay, is precisely the aimless, nonsensical, hilarious jest conceived by August Wilhelm. Both plays assume the fundamental prerogative which the Schlegels claimed for comic caprice: to override all laws of experience and reason, together with the corollary prerogatives of implausibility, incoherence, and mockery of theatrical illusion. However, *Der gestiefelte Kater* alone exemplifies their further requirement of pure comedy, that the secondary satiric purpose be sublimated in the esthetic impression of jesting play. Likewise, this is the only one of Tieck's comedies which actually succeeds to a considerable extent in communicating the poet's jesting spirit to the reader, although even here the impression is marred by intellectual pedantry and excessive concentration upon a single comic motif.

Tieck's comedies fall more seriously short of the Schlegels' comic ideals in the range of materials covered by their jest and satire. The world which they ridicule is not the whole, vital universe of human folly and animality which the Schlegels rightly credited to Aristophanes, but a petty theatrical, belletristic milieu with trivial, ephemeral foibles. Except in the stylized literary satire of *Däumchen*, Tieck avoids the most pungently comical aspect of the human animal, his sexual appetite, dealing rather with such harmless cravings as those of a fairy-tale king for rabbits and raisins, of a cat for nightingales, of philistines for beer.

The disparity becomes much greater when we turn aside from the Schlegels' theoretical abstraction and judge Tieck's fantastic comedy by direct comparison with the work of Aristophanes. Aristophanes was the great exponent of a great age, and he aimed his satiric darts at targets worthy of his mettle: the historically crucial political and diplomatic tendencies of Athens; the literary, philosophical, and educational revolutions in progress there in his time; the titanic personalities of Cleon, Euripides, and Socrates. More than this, the satire of Aristophanes is of universal significance as the foremost example of that hard-bitten ethical conservatism which rises up in every complex civilization to lament the rugged virtues of a simpler past. His own personal stature and that of his adversaries, the timeless appeal of his satiric perspective, and the inexhaustible vitality of his comic and poetic fantasy make him supreme among all comic poets and the one truly great creator of farcical fantastic comedy in the history of world literature.

Measured against this standard, Tieck appears as a facile, whimsical littérateur, who could not achieve truly universal poetic creation or even discern what was most significant in his own age. His audience was not a cosmopolitan nation assembled in its annual festival but a circle of sophisticates sipping tea in the literary salon. The arena of political satire was closed to him by the strict Prussian censorship, but even had it not been, neither his own interests nor those of his public would have led him to it. Not only have the targets of Tieck's theatrical, literary, and cultural satire, the Ifflands, Nicolais, Falks, and Böttigers, passed into oblivion, but the conflict itself appears insignificant after the passage of only a century and a half. Whereas Aristophanes championed a great old national tradition against a great new one, Tieck was attacking a moribund and largely imitative culture, German Rationalism, on behalf of a richer and more original new movement, German Romanticism, which was nevertheless itself destined to early decay. Tieck ignores the one vital exponent of the German Enlightenment, Lessing, and toward his conflict with its minor adherents, the real literary and intellectual leaders of the time held either a position of neutrality (Kant, Herder, and Schiller) or at best one of sympathetic nonbelligerence (Goethe). Tieck's later attack against Goethe's own classicism passed virtually unnoticed by both its object and the public.

Tieck stands comparison with Aristophanes as a comic poet scarcely better than as a satirist. On the one hand we see noth-

ing more than an innocuous, childish whimsy, on the other, the
hearty, lusty jest of vigorous manhood. The relative weakness
of Tieck's comedy does not result solely from his renunciation of
the powerful appeal of sexual jest. The ludicrous effects of
Aristophanic comedy were also intensified by heavy blows of
personal ridicule, by modern standards often aimed below the
belt; Tieck scrupulously confined his personal thrusts to literary,
theatrical, and intellectual areas.[160] Another reason why his
comic fantasy appears childish is that the want of an adult
mythological tradition compelled him to draw his best materials
from the fairy tale. (Such other substitutes as the artificially
resuscitated ancient mythology of *Die verkehrte Welt* and the
Oriental fantasy borrowed secondhand, through Gozzi, for *Zerbino* proved much less satisfactory.) Above all, Aristophanes
dwarfs Tieck in his comic inventiveness, his breathless succession
of hilarious incongruities, and his alternation of the purely
ludicrous with a lyric poetry rich in beautiful sound and imagery,
yet still comical.

When we apply the Schlegels' theory of pure fantastic comedy
to each of these poets, we find that Aristophanic comedy deviates
from it both for traditional reasons and because of the transcending genius of its creator, whereas Tieck's deviations disclose
themselves as real artistic defects. Each poet satisfies the demand for a sustained impression of mirth in only one comedy,
Aristophanes in *The Birds* and Tieck in *Der gestiefelte Kater*.
More commonly Aristophanes interrupts his jest with serious
polemics, and this not merely in the interlude of the parabasis.
The unity of mood theoretically attributed to his comedies by the
Schlegels is thus actually broken, but his unique genius, personality, and convictions supply their own unity. When the lesser
artist, Tieck, adulterates his fantastic farce with a pedantic
enumeration of rationalistic institutions, with tiring allegories,
sentimental idylls, and saccharine lyricism, nothing is offered to
replace the unity of spirit which he has suspended. The Schlegels'
theory of a pure fantastic comedy does not afford a balanced
critical appraisal of Aristophanes, but its validity for a poet of
more limited resources is attested by the superiority of those
works, *Der gestiefelte Kater* and *Rotkäppchen,* in which Tieck
achieves the most uniform evocation of a jesting spirit. And
even with Aristophanes, one may question whether any of the

more polemic works has stood the test of time as well as *The Birds.*

Although Friedrich and August Wilhelm Schlegel did not appreciate the entire poetic, theatrical, and human greatness of Aristophanes, they did discover the essential principles of his comic art, and they correctly differentiated its form, characterization, and relation to ordinary human experience from those of the realistic and relatively dignified comedy which dominated the European theater from Menander to Goldoni. Tieck, before he knew of the Schlegels' discovery and probably before he had acquired any intimate familiarity of his own with Aristophanes, embodied in *Der gestiefelte Kater* a number of the same comic principles: the preference of hilarious laughter over the delicate smile; the exploitation of the irrational, the supernatural, and the outlandishly implausible; the grotesque caricature; the inconsequent and the inconsequential action; and the incoherent structure.[161] In spite of Tieck's vast inferiority as a comic artist to Aristophanes, one cannot help noticing the similarity of comic technique, a similarity which is most impressive precisely in those comedies where there is the least reason to suspect direct imitation.

Virtually all of the fantastic devices characteristic of *Der gestiefelte Kater* and *Die verkehrte Welt* (the comedies written by Tieck when he had the least familiarity with Aristophanes) are to be encountered in Attic comedy. The Frogs, Birds, Wasps, who give their names to three of the comedies are grotesque combinations of human and bestial properties. The Empusa in *The Frogs* is a protean monster. The Clouds are objectified metaphors with the multiple identity of meteorological phenomena, mythological beings, and symbols of logical confusion, and the Wasps are at once insects and parasitic jurors. Tieck's Hanswurst and theatrical Innkeeper, who are individual characters and theatrical institutions at the same time, have their prototype in Mnesilochus living through a number of Euripidean roles in the embarrassment of his captivity at the Thesmophorian Festival.

Tieck's favorite device of irrational comedy, the mockery of theatrical illusion, is also put to effective and varied use by Aristophanes, though without the laborious complexity and one-sided concentration which we have observed in the German dramatist. The parabasis, in which the Chorus harangues the audience on the poet's behalf, is not a case in point, for it usually consists of direct polemics or of pleading for the judges' prize. This is an anticipated interlude in theatrical illusion rather than a sudden interruption, and it serves other than comic purposes. However, in all of the Aristophanic comedies, characters as well as the Chorus either directly address the spectators or allude to them and the stage equipment. These infractions of theatrical representation are momentary incidents, but their comic effect is all the greater for their suddenness and brevity. The comedy of allusion to the audience is frequently spiced by derogatory connotations. Thus *The Frogs* opens with Xanthias asking his master, Dionysus, whether he should "crack any of those old jokes . . . at which the audience never fail to laugh,"[162] and a little later Dionysus himself points out among the audience the parricides and perjurors who Heracles said would be met in Hades (274-5). In *The Knights,* Demosthenes tells the Sausage-Seller that the "brightest in the tiers" will stand beside him in his fight with Paphlagon (228).

Aristophanic characters also make numerous references to the stage and its equipment: Socrates points out the arrival of the Clouds "by the Entrance" to the orchestra (*Clouds* 326)[163] and Peisthetaerus instructs the stage hands in *The Birds* (656). The *eccyclema,* a machine for rolling the scene around, is the subject of allusions in *The Knights* (1249), *The Acharnians* (408),[164] and *The Thesmophoriazusae* (96). One of the choicer jests on stage machinery is the plea made by Trygaeus in *The Peace* (174-6) as he flies toward Olympus on a dungbeetle:

> I say, scene-shifter, have a care of me,
> You gave me quite a turn; and if you don't
> Take care, I'm certain I shall feed my beetle.

This might be compared to Scaramuccio's request in *Die verkehrte Welt* that the Machinist keep him from being soaked in the sea of trapdoors.[165] Characters in several Aristophanic comedies comment on their costumes and masks; the Chorus of *The Frogs,* for example, complains of the "cheapness" which compels it to wear torn costumes (404). Dramatic literature and theatrical institutions are, of course, the principal subject of discussion in *The Frogs* and a favorite topic in other comedies as well.

The confusion of the material portrayed and the process of theatrical portrayal is thus seen to be a frequent source of Aristophanic jest, but the play as a whole is never concentrated or built up on this single device as in *Der gestiefelte Kater* and *Die verkehrte Welt*. What with Aristophanes is a momentary confusion becomes in these two comedies of Tieck an inextricable fusion. What with Aristophanes is one of many comic spices, Tieck serves up in these two plays as the main dish.

In Tieck's later comedies, which make less use of the play upon theatrical representation, other Aristophanic devices become more prominent. His puns on personal names in *Anti-Faust* are an obvious imitation of Aristophanes, and those in *Prinz Zerbino* may be inspired by the same source. The incorporation of a number of these puns in the satiric allegories of the Mill and Forge in the latter play remind us of the procession of allegorical figures, each associated with a contemporary of Aristophanes, in *The Birds* (274 ff.). These allegories of *Zerbino*, the cask episode in *Anti-Faust*, and Semmelziege's "flights of fancy" from the giant's springboard in *Däumchen*[166] come closer to the objectified metaphor used by Aristophanes in the titular themes of *The Clouds* and *The Wasps* than do any of the devices of *Der gestiefelte Kater* and *Die verkehrte Welt*. In *Däumchen*, Tieck not only makes his sole venture into the territory of sex, but also carries out his only extensive parody of tragic literary style in comic situations, the device used with such telling effect against Euripides in *The Frogs, The Thesmophoriazusae,* and *The Acharnians*. If it were simply a question of detailed parallels with Aristophanic technique, Tieck's later comedies might appear more nearly Aristophanic than *Der gestiefelte Kater*. *Zerbino*, completed during Tieck's period of closest contact with the Schlegels, and *Däumchen*, written some time afterwards, may well have been directly influenced by Aristophanes. But in Tieck's one candid imitation of Aristophanes, *Anti-Faust*, we have striking evidence that this influence was not really fruitful. Unable either to sustain the spirit of Aristophanic jest or combine it with a comic spirit of his own, Tieck quickly lapsed here into his fatal belletristic pedantry and then completely abandoned the unhappy enterprise. The more spontaneous fantastic comic style of Tieck at his best, which we find in *Der gestiefelte Kater*, gives this single farce claim to a humble kinship with the Attic master.

CHAPTER FIVE
Tieck's Esthetic Thought

Although Tieck was no esthetic theorist and lacked both the brilliant critical insight of Friedrich Schlegel and the thorough, orderly exposition of August Wilhelm, his criticism is significant as an attempt to explain the general artistic aims of his own creation to his reading public, as evidence of his reaction to tendencies in the contemporary literature and theater, and frequently, as in the case of his critical essays on Shakespeare and the Elizabethan theater, for the esthetic standards which he applies to the evaluation of comedy.

Tieck's utterances on comedy fall into three distinct periods which in a measure reflect the tendencies of his own creation. The criticism prior to 1797, consisting primarily of the first draft of his fragmentary *Buch über Shakespeare*,[1] uses realistic and largely rationalistic principles, tinged with a superficial Kantian influence, to appraise the comic elements in Shakespeare. Here Tieck is concerned with the portrayal of the ludicrous as it is observed in actual life. His turn toward the more subjective critical principles characteristic of Romantic thought took place about 1797 in the brief second draft of the work cited,[2] which may have been written after he came in contact with the Schlegels. In this phase, which lasted until 1811, Tieck's thought is centered upon the mood expressed by the comic poet, and he is interested in two kinds of comic expression: one consisting wholly of intoxicated, nonsensical jest and another in which comic and serious elements alternate. After 1811, Tieck's critical utterances reflect a curious dichotomy: In so far as they deal with other modern writers they show a swing back to conventional realistic criteria, but to his own creations he continues to apply the subjective standards of his Romantic phase.[3]

A demarcation between Tieck's creative and critical writings is sometimes impossible, particularly for the period from 1797 to 1811, with which we are principally concerned. Some of his most significant pronouncements on the objectives of comedy are found within his comedies themselves, in the prose frame through which these are introduced in *Phantasus* (1811), and in the dramatic allegory *Der Autor* (1800).[4] On the other hand, the critical *Briefe über Shakespeare* (1800) has something of a literary form. The more strictly critical sources include the posthumously published "Bemerkungen über Parteilichkeit, Dummheit und Bosheit,"[5] written in 1800, the first part of the essay on "Das altenglische Theater" (1811),[6] and the second and third drafts of *Das Buch über Shakespeare,* which H. Lüdeke, the editor, dates, respectively, after 1796 and *circa* 1800.[7]

The transition in all aspects of Tieck's criticism from Rationalistic objectivity to Romantic subjectivity is a belated recognition of tendencies which had appeared sporadically in his creative writing from its very beginnings and were already well established there by 1796 in *Hanswurst als Emigrant, Ein Prolog, William Lovell,* and the first volume of the *Volksmärchen.* But the year 1797 also marks a special epoch in the history of Tieck's personal disposition and temperament which made possible his creation of fantastic comedy and determined the tenor of his subsequent utterances on jest and satire. This was probably the happiest and emotionally most wholesome year of Tieck's entire lifetime. Conflicts which had shortly before expressed themselves inwardly in haunting terror, feelings of guilt, and solipsism *(Der blonde Eckbert, William Lovell),* outwardly in disillusionment, cynicism, and contempt for the culture of his day *(Die Teegesellschaft),* were now temporarily surmounted in a mood of jesting merriment expressed through playful ridicule: "That which had been oppressing me in my youth, the repugnant elements of the age that had disturbed me . . . , now came into view . . . on the magic canvas of poetry. Serene jest was compelled to seize upon these images in gentle fun . . ."[8]

The most striking difference between Tieck's utterances pertinent to comedy and those of the Schlegels is Tieck's distaste for classification under categories, which extended to the avoidance even of such terms as *Komödie* and *Lustspiel.* Tieck, therefore, cannot be said to have a theory of comedy, but in his discussion of particular comedies he does reveal very decided views on the spirit in which such works are or should be written, their form, their characterization, and so forth. It is these tastes and preferences of Tieck which we shall be comparing with the concepts and theories of the Schlegels. We shall also have to dispense with the convenient starting point which Friedrich and August Wilhelm afforded in their exaltation of Aristophanes. Tieck mentions the Attic dramatist rather infrequently, not always altogether favorably, and prior to 1800 in such general terms as to indicate only the most superficial acquaintance. A suggestion that his own work lacks the polemic bitterness and political tendentiousness of Aristophanic comedy is the only comparison that occurs to him;[9] he never associates his own comedies with those of Aristophanes as examples of a peculiar poetic category. Nevertheless, there is an unmistakable similarity between Tieck's preferences in the comic domain and the esthetic concepts which the Schlegels developed from the Old Attic Comedy.

The Romantic concern for the mood of literary creations first appears in the notes constituting the second draft of *Das Buch über Shakespeare,* where Tieck makes "poetic mood" one of the main headings of his investigation and contrasts it with mere "portrayal of the world."[10] The mood which attracted him most at this period is described thirty years later in one of the prefaces to his collected works:

> Formerly I had perhaps set too high a score on the portrayal of passion, knowledge of the heart and of all human aberrations and failings . . . ; now my interest and study were inspired by the totality, by graciousness and *jest,* by the deep wisdom of the [fictive] invention, and by that *wanton insanity* which often annihilates its own laws. The *play* of art, the noble *lightheartedness of joy,* no doubt momentarily obscured for me again the grandeur of passion and the portrayal of deep spiritual anguish in Shakespeare and Sophocles.[11]

Whereas at the beginning of his Shakespeare studies Tieck had occupied himself with the ludicrous and the comic in situations and characters,[12] the objects of comic portrayal, he is now concerned with the laughter of the poet and of his readers or spectators. It is all-important to him whether the spirit animating that laughter is a rapturous joy overflowing with love and goodwill or a derisive, intimidating mockery. To quote one of the characters whose dialogue makes up the frame of *Phantasus:*

> The ludicrous which is associated with the contemptible and which so many poets have tried to use for the persecution and possible destruction of this or that so-called folly . . . is hateful and bitter . . . ; and I gladly confess that I have never been able to derive any joy or amusement from these so-called satirists, especially of modern times, nor do I know whether I have actually laughed at their portrayals. . . . But how different is . . . the delight of joy, the rapture of our whole soul, . . . when all our perceptions and recollections are submerged for a time in that wondrous whirlpool of ecstasy which lets the tones of laughter sound up from their hidden depths.[13]

We have already seen Tieck associate this joyous rapture with play, and here too he goes on to praise "that innocence of the comic, . . . that light touching of all objects, that good-natured play with all creatures and their thoughts and feelings" in Shakespeare.[14] Tieck calls his own satiric comedies "frolics of serene, untroubled whimsy."[15] The Author in his allegorical Shrovetide play, under the influence of his Muse, is so completely given over to joy that he makes "merry play" even of suffering and vexation.[16]

The joy animating such comic creation must be completely self-contained. It plays without concern for any effect upon the external world, without interest in the betterment of other people.[17] The jesting spirit to which the poet abandons himself is so light that it needs neither the "stone foundation" of a didactic aim nor any other prosaic, external application.[18] Tieck repeatedly contrasts this ideal of volatile, aimless jest with bitter satire and with all such didactic or moralizing comedy as he found in the contemporary German theater. In his *Denkwürdige Geschichtschronik der Schildbürger* (1796) he describes his Schildburgers, who caricature rationalistic Germans at the end of the eighteenth century, as too high-minded to use the theater as anything but a kind of "annex to the hospital," where they might purge themselves of their failings. For them it was not "a kind of play of fantasy or a place where one passed the time with amusing farces, but a veritable school of morals. The Schildburgers were so exacting in this that they simply could not stand plays in which they unexpectedly had to laugh . . ."[19] Just as the Playwright in *Der gestiefelte Kater* protested against didactic solemnity in the theater,[20] the Author of the Shrovetide play deplores the habitual public demand:

> Das Lächerliche soll aber nicht sein lächerlich pur,
> Sondern drinn stecken eine Erbaulichkeit . . .[21]

Nevertheless, Tieck believes that everything in comic jest must have its serious connotations, just as everything earnest has its laughable aspect, that laughter and tears can be conjoined, and that we can laugh at people whom we love.[22] This idea is not necessarily at variance with his and the Schlegels' conception of a pure jest. August Wilhelm differentiated the serious purpose underlying the comedies of Aristophanes from the esthetic impression of purposiveness created by modern didactic comedy,[23] and Tieck makes a similar distinction in the word-symphony which introduces *Die verkehrte Welt:* "Earnest eventually seeks jest; jest again tires and seeks earnest. But . . . *if one injects too much design and purpose into either,* then both true earnest and true merriment are all too easily lost."[24]

Even though he related laughter to tears, Tieck rejected sentimental comedy no less emphatically than did the Schlegels. He has the rationalist Nestor in the Garden of Poesy, in reply to a question by Ariosto, indignantly deny that there is anything funny about the German comedies of his age: "What on earth are you thinking of? Well, anyone can see how coarse your time was. Our [comedies] touch one to tears; they're all full of preachers and princes, villains and lofty, noble people."[25] To sum up Tieck's view—and that of German Romanticism in general—on the relation of jest, earnest, and sentiment, any literary expression of pure jest will spontaneously communicate overtones of earnest thought and sorrowful emotion, but there is no place in poetic art for didacticism or calculated tear-jerking.

Tieck also agrees with the Schlegels that the rapturous intoxication of jest is incompatible with rational order and probability:

> In what intoxication does our spirit exult, once granted the power to see arising within itself, constantly renewed and rejuvenated, a thousand changing, colorful, hovering, dancing figures. . . . The soul envelops itself in songs of all colors and rejoices to the heavens that it will long be free from dull, everyday life.
>
> As a golden spark kindles fireworks . . . , so that the intoxicated eye watches with enchantment the swirl of changing colored flames: so it is with the vacillating, radiant images which joy displays to us.[26]

The incidental "music" to *Die verkehrte Welt,* from which this last rhapsody is taken, tells us elsewhere that the "good confusion" of such a comedy is "worth more than a bad order."[27]

Tieck therefore finds it natural to follow the Schlegels in setting up the Aristophanic "intoxication of fantasy" with its seemingly childish, inane plots as "pure comedy" over against the ordered, serious, and therefore "degenerate" comedy of Plautus.[28] He sees a parallel contrast between the "real poetry" of Shakespeare and the lifeless intellectual composition of Ben Jonson,[29] who had previously fascinated Tieck sufficiently to inspire his adaptation of *Volpone*[30] and whose *Epicoene*[31] he translated in 1800. Jonson is the most perfect example of all that "keen-minded moderns have sought to produce by motivation, arrangement, development, and necessary connection," only to show us how far a false path can lead.[32] For similar reasons *Der Autor* ridicules the plausible realism of comedy in Tieck's own time:

> Sie wollen lachen mit Natur,
> Und über eine Wahrscheinlichkeit . . .[33]

The nearest thing to a structural principle which Tieck recognizes for creations like *Der gestiefelte Kater* and *Die verkehrte Welt* is a "circular path" that leads us back to where we started. This metaphor, applied in *Phantasus*,[34] recalls the "dissolving into nothingness" that delighted August Wilhelm Schlegel in comedies of intrigue.[35]

The mark of the Schlegels is again evident when Tieck proclaims the license of comedy to exploit human sensuality and argues that any recognition of propriety by Aristophanes would have shackled his comic caprice.[36] Tieck blames the squeamishness of his own contemporaries on their inward degradation. The danger of moral corruption lay, not in a frank portrayal of the animal in man's dual nature, but in that subtle attempt to deny —or reduce to purely physical elements—his spiritual side, which Tieck found in such modern writers as Claude Crébillon and Wieland.[37]

Two passages in Tieck's writings come closer than any others to a definition of the kind of comedy which he preferred and would have liked to consider exemplified in *Der gestiefelte Kater* and *Die verkehrte Welt*. These sum up the qualities discussed above and also allude to the two other characteristics which have monopolized the attention of Tieck's critics: his satire and his upsetting of theatrical illusion. One passage is from the posthumously published essay directed against the satire of Tieck's literary adversaries, Falk, Merkel, and Beck:

> That there may be a kind of wit that plays within itself and accepts the possibility, indeed necessity, *of regarding the whole age and everything happening in it as jesting play*, and that the right kind of jest simply consists in believing in nothing earnest, . . . of this he [Falk] could, of of course, not be aware . . .[38]

The other is uttered by the character who introduces *Der gestiefelte Kater* in *Phantasus*:

> I offer you today all that I have of this kind, an airy composition *which is all froth and light jest*, and you must not take it more seriously than it is intended. Yet *one cannot easily jest about the theater without jesting about the world* at the same time . . .[39]

The two most striking hallmarks of Tieck's fantastic comedy were thus seen by its creator as inevitable manifestations of the pervading spirit of light, jesting play.

Turning first to Tieck's conception of comic satire, we note that he would exclude personal satire in the sense of a "hateful accusation" but attributed a vital comic function to the fantastic exaggeration of personal traits in individuals. He used this principle to justify the Aristophanic caricature of Socrates: "That fantasy exaggerates in its delight is self-evident, for otherwise its portrayal would not be poetic . . ."[40] Protesting against the satire of himself and the Schlegels in Beck's *Camäleon*, Tieck nevertheless asserted that they would gladly be the objects of the right kind of personal satire: "For if one found me and others worthy of being made ludicrous, if we were to serve the public as examples, then we could not take exception to happy additions, hyperboles, great, striking features, because without these an individual image cannot be elevated to universality."[41] He even provided his satirist with specific suggestions: Tieck and his friends should be presented on the stage in ludicrous contrast to their surrounding world and to simple, common-sense characters, who would vainly seek some trace of sense in their writings and would parody their poetic creation. The personal traits actually selected by Beck, on the other hand, were not literary eccentricities but alleged moral vices. In such caricature, Tieck protested both the assault upon his probity as a citizen and the failure to lend universal significance to the distorted traits. Even worse, the spirit of this satire was not comic but moralizing.[42]

The universality which Tieck demanded of satire was twofold: the investment of particular character traits with universal significance by means of fanciful exaggeration, and the encompassing of all the follies of the age as material for laughter. His criticism stresses this second, horizontal dimension of universality as much as the first: "Never before has there been a period in which the world with all its endeavors and events was such a parody of itself as the present. Formerly it sufficed to satirize a person or a state institution, and it never occurred even to the daring Aristophanes, who spares neither gods nor men, to present his whole age comically . . . Now, however, we have come to the point where we must laugh at everything or at nothing . . ."[43]

Tieck's conception of universality suffers from a fallacy we have already encountered in August Wilhelm Schlegel. Neither the variety of follies exhibited nor the degree to which they are exaggerated by fantasy determines the universality of satire, but rather the significance of its objects for humanity as a whole and the timeless validity of the viewpoint from which they are presented. Failure to recognize this principle not only limited Tieck's appreciation of Aristophanic satire but led him to praise indiscriminately that parody of "the world with all its events and people" which the German folk theater had offered through traditional clowns like Hanswurst.[44]

From Tieck's standpoint, satiric jest could not be universal unless the stage itself were among the cultural phenomena of which it made sport, and to this end the convention of an inviolable theatrical illusion had to be sacrificed. Like other Romanticists, Tieck felt that such illusion was "demanded too much in the drama." He would recognize no more literal illusion than the esthetic satisfaction of comparing reality with its representation, which is in no danger of destruction;[45] he protests against the sacrosanct law of illusion which has been set up in the modern drama, and suggests that there may be "various kinds of illusion" and works of art "in which illusion does not constitute the first condition, the principal law."[46] He regards the jest at the expense of theatrical portrayal as a phenomenon naturally attendant upon the development of the theater and justifies his own use of the device in *Der gestiefelte Kater* by the precedents of Aristophanes and Shakespeare:

> . . . with the development of the theater there develops also the jest about the theater, as we already observe in Aristophanes; he can scarcely forbear treating himself ironically, . . . because the twofold nature, the duality of the human mind, the wonderful contradiction within us, provides the basis of the comic stage. The curious aim of the theater to present a story before us with the greatest vividness has more than once been treated ironically by Shakespeare in tragedy, where at one moment he passes off his play as truth and in contradiction to this derides the stage from the stage itself as a lie and a weak imitation. He had to be very sure of himself not to fear that destruction of illusion which is foreseen by almost all modern textbooks of the art when the theater is mentioned in the theater.[47]

The use of the verb *ironisieren,* "to treat ironically," in the
above passage of *Phantasus* is Tieck's sole association of the destruction of illusion with irony, for when the same verb is used
on another occasion (in describing the performance of a wandering troupe)[48] only an unconscious irony in the usual sense is
involved. The passage quoted dates from 1811, when Tieck was,
of course, acquainted with Friedrich Schlegel's conception of
literary irony; but Tieck does not mention Schlegel here, as he
very frequently does when he elaborates upon *Ironie* itself, and
the reference to the *Ironisieren* in Shakespeare shows how Tieck
could also derive this use of the term from the commonplace
meaning of irony without thinking of Schlegel's concept. At all
events, this one equivocal and fleeting association of some sort
of irony with the violation of theatrical illusion hardly makes
Tieck responsible for the subsequent distortion of Friedrich
Schlegel's irony in literary history. The verbal derivative
ironisieren would be appropriate only to a device or technique,
as Tieck applies it here. We have already seen that, when he is
concerned with the spirit of his fantastic comedies, he always
speaks of joy, intoxication, jest, play, or whimsy, and shall
shortly observe also that when he speaks of *Ironie,* he generally
conceives it as a mood, perspective, or attitude in the sense of
Friedrich or August Wilhelm Schlegel, citing literary manifestations quite different from the destruction of illusion. We must
also bear in mind that what is *ironisiert* according to the passage
in question is not the dramatist's poetic creation but merely the
stage and its convention. Tieck clearly did not mean that either
he or Aristophanes—to say nothing of Shakespeare—was destroying the unifying poetic impression of his own work by this
mockery of theatrical representation.

When we approach the subject of comic characterization, we
find the most striking reversal of critical perspective between
the first and second drafts of *Das Buch über Shakespeare*. The
first draft expresses a decided preference for the individualized
characters of Shakespeare over his more generalized clowns and
fools, and demands that the comic characters be plausible and
true to life.[49] Although the young critic approved of Falstaff, he
thought that there should be limits to the wit and intellectual
superiority displayed by a comic character, and he sometimes
found these exceeded by Shakespeare.[50] For the most part, he

favored Shakespeare's unwittingly ludicrous figures, in short, that same "comic of observation" which wins such a cool reception from August Wilhelm Schlegel. However, in the second draft of this work and in his other writings from 1797 on, Tieck favors the fantastically exaggerated comic type, the caricature, or the mask;[51] his preferences in comic characterization have thus come around to the position of August Wilhelm.

These new standards of Tieck's Romantic period account for his partiality to the clowns of the German popular theater and puppet show, manifested in the introduction of a Hanswurst into two of his own fantastic comedies. In his critical writings we find repeated warm references to this type and to the kindred Lipperle, as he saw them presented by roving troupes and marionette theaters, whether for comic relief in serious melodrama or as major roles in farces.[52]

Tieck's approval of farce is reflected by the hostility of his rationalistic Schildburgers, who even banish marionettes from their city for enacting farces.[53] Sometimes Tieck applies the term farce (Posse or Possenspiel) to his own comic creation, as when his allegorical Author describes the product of his inspiration:

> Ich seh nur Masken um mich tanzen,
> Ein fröhliches Possenspiel wird aus dem Ganzen.[54]

The Playwright in Der gestiefelte Kater uses the plural Possen (translated "jokes" in the quotation above, p. 60, but connoting any farcical actions or utterances) to explain the means by which he had hoped to amuse his audience. Surely, if Tieck had been compelled to select from the various categories of comedy distinguished by August Wilhelm Schlegel the most suitable designation for his own Gestiefelter Kater and Verkehrte Welt, his choice would have been the Posse.

Alongside the purely comical, or farcical, expression of intoxicated jest, Tieck's criticism, particularly at the end of his Romantic phase, reflects interest in a mixed tragicomic drama. In Tieck's own creation this interest is manifest over a much longer period, extending from Blaubart (1796) to Fortunat (1816). In fact, when we view Tieck's dramatic creation as a whole, the unadulterated comedy to which he aspired in Der gestiefelte Kater and Die verkehrte Welt appears no more than a fleeting interlude. The German Romanticists generally conceived the seriocomic drama as one transcending the limits of the stage, and the tendency toward closet drama also dominates most of Tieck's creation and criticism. A dialogue in *Phantasus* emphasizes the gradual transition between *Novelle* and drama, suggests that some of Shakespeare's comedies are on the border line, and concludes: " . . . a kind of poetry is undoubtedly permissible that cannot use even the best theater but erects in fantasy a stage for fantasy and attempts compositions which may perhaps be lyric, epic, and dramatic at the same time, gain a scope more or less denied to the novel, and assume liberties not appropriate to any other [kind of] dramatic poem."[55]

This discussion in *Phantasus* is touched off by a reference to a play of Lope de Vega. In his essay on "Das altenglische Theater," Tieck discusses the seriocomic drama of the Spanish Golden Age together with that of Elizabethan England, and like the Schlegels, he applies the adjective "romantic" to both. As qualities common to these two national traditions he mentions "the mixture of the comic and serious, the diversity of episodes, and the preference for materials from the rich and poetic national history."[56] Spanish romantic drama is distinguished by its "religious mood" combined with a pervading idealistic "enthusiasm," and by the variety and musical quality of its meters. It has one characteristic form, which reaches its highest development in Calderón. The Elizabethan drama uses language closer to prose, strives for historical clarity, and experiments with a variety of forms. In the Spanish drama "the tragic and comic are strictly separated, and even though the irony of the poet often hovers over his wild and passionate scenes, the passion of his characters remains completely poetic and sublime. The Englishman, on the other hand, is fond of mixing, into even the highest flight of passion, something strange which borders on the comic and often injects irony into the core of pain and suffering . . ." The relatively simple formal composition developed by Calderón is susceptible of exact imitation. This would be a hopeless undertaking in the case of Shakespeare, each of whose plays has its unique complex form.[57]

One such attempt at an exact imitation of the structural principles of Calderonian romantic drama was made by Tieck himself in his *Kaiser Octavianus* (1801-2), and in the experiment he also incorporated the epic scope and some motifs of plot from

Shakespeare's *Winter's Tale* and *Cymbeline.* This most representative attempt of German Romanticism to re-create its conception of romantic drama counterpoises the nostalgic exaltation of medieval Christian chivalry presented in its serious characters with a variety of earthy, prosaic comic figures. Like *Prinz Zerbino,* it combines epic, lyric, and dramatic elements, but the total impression is one of a novel in dialogue form. The imitation of Calderón is especially evident in a variety of rhymed and assonant verse forms.[58] Statements which Tieck made to Solger that *Octavianus,* unlike his tragedy *Genoveva,* was not the product of spontaneous inspiration but of deliberate design *(Absicht),*[59] confirm the internal evidence that this play is a conscious effort to exemplify the Schlegels' notion of *romantic comedy.*

We have just seen Tieck apply the term *irony,* precisely in the manner of August Wilhelm Schlegel, to the romantic dramas of Shakespeare and Calderón. Tieck does not explicitly mention irony prior to his acquaintance with the Schlegels, and then when he does enunciate the concept, their influence is unmistakable. After 1808 another influence is added, that of Karl W. F. Solger, but the latter's conception of irony is close to that of Friedrich Schlegel, which it clarified rather than displaced in Tieck's thought. However, irony also has its roots in Tieck himself antedating these influences, even though not as a conscious theory. In such early writings as *William Lovell, Der blonde Eckbert, Blaubart,* and *Ein Prolog,* all written before Tieck knew the Schlegels, we encounter a feeling that nothing, not even one's own existence, can be accepted as real, that there are indeed no distinct boundaries between reality, illusion, and fantasy. The similarity between this mood of the young Tieck[60] and the relativism or "cynicism" of Friedrich Schlegel's ironic philosophy is so great, that either one could serve as the source for some slightly later utterances of Tieck, such as the following "musical" motif in an interlude of *Die verkehrte Welt:*

> Every time a philosopher meets a surprise, whenever there is something he does not understand, . . . he cries out: there is no sense [*Verstand*] in this! Yes, when reason [*Verstand*] really tries to get to the bottom of itself and probes its own innermost nature, when it observes itself and can see how it observes, then it says: there is no sense in this![61]

However, the irony of which Tieck comes to speak expressly is a more temperate recognition of the relativity, imperfection, and incongruity of everything human. He points this out in one of those puppet plays of which he is so fond, where a nobleman of excellent character unexpectedly reveals a childish human weakness,[62] and he mentions also the "sympathetic, loving irony" with which human frailties are portrayed by Cervantes and Shakespeare.[63] Although such references to irony are sparse in Tieck's Romantic period, they show that, prior to his contact with Solger, he associated the concept with the interplay of jest and earnest in "romantic drama" and with the portrayal of human incongruities.

Some critics have found a conscious application of irony only in the works which Tieck wrote after his contact with Solger: the two *Fortunat* tragedies and the *Novellen*. But irony in the sense of Friedrich Schlegel, and particularly those aspects of it which August Wilhelm Schlegel associated with romantic drama, are clearly exemplified in *Kaiser Octavianus*. Earthy comic figures not only appear in ironic contrast to idealized romantic heroes, but present a deliberate, if at times subtle, parody of them. The very exaggeration of the idealistic, chivalrous characters and the ludicrous implausibility of the exotic plot suggest that Tieck did not take the serious side of his play in dead earnest, but there are even more unmistakable indications. The heroic figures are made to appear ludicrous when they step outside their world of religious and chivalrous idealism into the realm of earthy utilitarian sagacity inhabited by the comic figures. Occasionally these last call our attention to some particularly glaring implausibility in the preceding action, or parody the elaborate versification in which their heroic counterparts express themselves. Such devices weaken, but do not wholly destroy, the somewhat nebulous representative illusion of this closet drama. They serve as reminders of the smiling irony with which the author must view the romantic idealism which he has objectified. Tieck is here emulating the "parody of the letter and . . . irony over the spirit of romantic drama" which Friedrich Schlegel attributed to Shakespeare.[64] This is one case in which the "Romantic irony" coined by literary criticism could be applied precisely in the sense in which the early German Romanticists understood each of its component terms.

Kaiser Octavianus, which Tieck calls a *Lustspiel*, might thus be described as an ironic romantic comedy. By the same token,

the double tragedy *Fortunat* may be termed an ironic romantic
drama. Although the balance is heavily shifted toward the side
of tragedy, there is still a very sharp contrast between the somber
portrayal of the principal characters and their destinies and the
farcical, but essentially realistic, comedy of the minor figures.
Apart from this contrast, the irony lies in the limitations which
render the tragic characters incapable of directing their destinies,
to the repeated frustration of their hopes and plans. This irony,
unlike that of *Octavianus*, resides wholly within the characters
and does not display the dramatist's attitude toward his work as
such. Poetic irony of this sort, which here is a direct application
of the philosophy of Solger,[65] had been anticipated in a few of
the examples cited by Friedrich Schlegel and in the majority of
August Wilhelm's examples of irony.[66]

One of Tieck's intellectual peculiarities is the length of time
which he required either to become critically conscious of his own
creative tendencies or to assimilate fully the esthetic ideas of
others. The artistic principles embodied in Tieck's comedies of
1797 find their first adequate enunciation in the *Phantasus* dialogues of 1811; the new comic realism which accompanied the
turn of the century in *Rotkäppchen* and *Octavianus* is reflected
in dramaturgical pronouncements of the 1820's; the influence of
the Schlegels upon Tieck's criticism remained superficial until
after his contacts with them had terminated. And so also the
poetic theories of Solger, exemplified in *Fortunat* and in prose
narratives written during the years of his association with Tieck,
are not fully digested in Tieck's criticism (the prefaces of his
Schriften and the conversations with Köpke) until long after
Solger's death.

We must therefore turn to pronouncements belonging to the
last twenty-five years of Tieck's long life for his most thoughtful
formulations of irony, in which he synthesizes the principles of
Solger and of Friedrich Schlegel. Solger had retained the fundamental concept of Schlegel's irony[67] but had given it a more rigid
formulation within the framework of his own philosophical system and drawn from it much more austere practical conclusions.
His philosophy distinguishes sharply between the absolute Idea
and the phenomenal world—for Solger only a "real nothingness"
—through which the Idea reveals itself. In the process of this
revelation, absolute reality takes on the limitations of phenome-

nal existence and thus in a sense destroys itself. The ironic poet
is one with a tragic awareness of this unceasing revelation and
annihilation of the Idea, both in external existence and in his own
artistic creation.[68]

The inferences which Solger would draw from this principle
for life and art were detachment, restraint, and a somber resignation to human weakness and self-frustration. To Friedrich
Schlegel, also, irony implied detachment and a kind of restraint,
but it also meant an urbane skepticism and a "liberality" which
could affirm everything and commit itself to nothing. Tieck's
late utterances on irony identify the fundamental concepts of
Solger and of Friedrich Schlegel without accepting the more
frivolous inferences sometimes drawn by the latter. Tieck speaks
of a "higher irony" in the sense of both Solger and Schlegel, and
distinguishes it from the commonplace irony which merely in-
tends the opposite of its words. Relating how the publisher,
Nicolai, had misunderstood "the perfectly simple irony, the reversal of the thing in which the bad is called good and the good
bad," in one of his early prose satires, Tieck goes on to ask:

> How, then, is the higher irony of Aristophanes, or even more, that of
> Shakespeare, to be comprehended . . . ? Or what are readers . . . to
> make of Socratic irony or of that irony which Solger proclaimed indis-
> pensable to any work of art . . . ? Over the whole of any Platonic dia-
> logue (take, for example, the *Symposium*) there hovers, after all, a
> higher, more spiritual irony than that which is expressed, say, in Soc-
> rates' apparent ignorance. And what would the critics or philosophers
> term that ultimate perfection of a poetic work of art, the warranty . . .
> of genuine inspiration, that ethereal spirit which has lovingly penetrated
> the work to its depths, yet hovers with artless satisfaction over the whole
> and (like the enjoying reader) can only create and comprehend it from
> this height? If we are not to call this perfection irony, like Solger or Fr.
> Schlegel (. . . in the *Athenäum*), then let some understanding person
> invent another name.[69]

Again, in a conversation with Köpke, Tieck protests against
the usual "one-sided," "prosaic," and "material" definitions of
irony and suggests "the Divinely Human in poetry" as the best
definition. In particular, the irony understood by Solger must
not be confused with "common irony, that coarse irony of Swift."
It "is not derision, scorn, persiflage," but "rather the deepest
earnest, which is at the same time joined with jest and true
mirth. . . . It is the power which gives the poet control over
his material; he is not to lose himself in it but to stand above it,

Thus irony keeps him from one-sidedness and empty idealization."[70]

These attempts of the older Tieck to define the irony of Solger turn out to be excellent paraphrases of the esoteric formulations long before given by Friedrich Schlegel in the 37th and 42nd *Fragmente* of the *Lyceum* and the 51st and 305th of the *Athenäum*.[71] It should be noted also that neither this "higher irony" of Schlegel and Solger nor the "common irony" of Swift is associated with the destruction of representative illusion. It is in the light of the passages quoted above that we may most safely interpret the brief differentiation of two kinds of irony in Tieck's own works contained in another conversation with Köpke: "In my own poetic works, irony is . . . at first more unconscious, yet definitely expressed; this is the case, above all, in *Lovell*. Direct irony prevails in *Der gestiefelte Kater;* something of the higher irony is found in *Blaubart,* and it is definitely present in *Fortunat*."[72] If the irony of *Fortunat* is the "higher" principle conceived by Friedrich Schlegel and Solger, then the "direct irony" of *Der gestiefelte Kater* must be of that "simple" or "common" variety which calls "the bad good and the good bad," for do not its characters enunciate the very poetic and theatrical values which its author would hold up to ridicule? There are surely better grounds for interpreting the passage in this light than there would be for identifying the *direkte Ironie* mentioned to Köpke with the *ironisieren* applied to jests about theatrical illusion a generation earlier in *Phantasus;* at all events, it is clear that the older Tieck attached no special significance to devices of this sort and did not confuse them with the irony of Friedrich Schlegel.

Tieck illustrates the kind of irony in which he is interested by examples from literature, none of which involves the destruction of illusion. He sees only "something analogous to irony" in Goethe but finds its supreme expression in Shakespeare and Cervantes, who were also important exponents of irony for Friedrich Schlegel.[73] For Tieck, the irony is primarily displayed by characters: Quixote, who strives to attain the noblest objectives through the most ludicrous methods; Brutus, who is too weak to accept the inevitable consequences of his own deed; and Hamlet, whose hesitations and actions alike bring about results opposite to those intended.[74]

Tieck's reference to the "higher irony of Aristophanes" has already been cited. Its meaning is explained in another relatively late critical utterance (1831), in which Tieck discards his earlier objection to Aristophanic bitterness:

> Aristophanes . . . was justified in viewing all the endeavors of his environment . . . as ludicrous and reprehensible, by ridiculing every disbelief and the sophistry of his day in his struggle to clear the ground for piety, civic responsibility, and patriotism. . . . His enthusiasm pulls us up to the heights on which he himself stands, and from here the world and its endeavors are revealed as silly and absurd, corrupt and wretched. Yet all these impressions are so sublimated in innocence and good feeling, that the polemics, the abasement of man, does not wound or pain us, but the art of the poet rather transports us into a state of true bliss. Through the power of this genuine irony we are placed on friendly terms with the inimical principle itself in the form of folly and nonsense. The inspired poet also incorporates into his merry picture some of the images and views which he champions, and he laughs in the happiest humor even at seriousness, virtue, and the gods . . . , without destroying the dignity of these objects in his absolutely unclouded merriment.[75]

The higher irony of Aristophanes thus consists in the sublimation of seriously motivated satiric ridicule in blissful merriment and the ability to make even the poet's own ideal the object of laughter. In this, his most mature appreciation of the Attic master, Tieck differs from the Schlegels only in reconciling a serious philosophical irony with the joyous merriment of pure comedy, as was possible for him now that he had learned from Solger to do greater justice than they to the underlying seriousness of Aristophanic jest.

CHAPTER SIX
The Schlegels and Tieck: Reactions and Influence

Among the various aspects of the mutual relationship between Tieck and the Schlegels, the two most pertinent to the present investigation are the influence which the Schlegels exerted upon Tieck's comic style and the reception which they accorded it. Other aspects need only brief mention: Regarding the influence of the Schlegels upon Tieck's own critical thinking, implicit in the foregoing chapter, one should distinguish between the help they gave him in recognizing his own innate tastes and creative practice, and their suggestion of new critical standards. Tieck's utterances on jest and satire fall under the first heading and are indebted to the Schlegels for little more than terminology. His appreciation of Aristophanic comedy was more largely a contribution of the Schlegels, but the lapse of decades and the further stimulus of Solger's philosophy were required before this influence was thoroughly assimilated in Tieck's thought. His concept of irony was partly a clarification of his own relationship toward life and art, partly another very slow assimilation of philosophical principles originating with Friedrich Schlegel and with Solger. As for the possibility of influence in the reverse direction, that of Tieck upon Friedrich Schlegel's conception of pure comedy is excluded by chronology, but August Wilhelm's criticism of comedy and farce was undoubtedly influenced by Tieck's examples, which August Wilhelm directly emulated in his own satire of Kotzebue.[1]

The most paradoxical outcome of our inquiry is that the one work by Tieck which comes closest to the Schlegels' conception of pure comedy, *Der gestiefelte Kater*, cannot have been influenced by their theory. It was already published by July, 1797;[2] Tieck did not make the acquaintance of Friedrich Schlegel before September of that year,[3] or of August Wilhelm until even later. The concentration of Tieck's early literary investigations upon the Elizabethan and modern periods makes it virtually certain that he would not have read Friedrich's essay on the Old Greek Comedy before becoming interested in the subject through personal contact with its author. A conscious attempt to exemplify Friedrich Schlegel's concept of irony in *Der gestiefelte Kater*,

such as might be inferred from some literary criticism, is altogether out of the question, for Schlegel's earliest *Fragmente*,
those of the *Lyceum*, were not sent to the publisher until September, 1797.[4] Tieck's unconscious illustration of Schlegel's
notion of a pure fantastic comedy results from the independent
development of similar inclinations in their two personalities
and from the ripeness of the general cultural environment for a
reaction against a pedantically prosaic and banally sentimental
theater.

Following the same paradoxical pattern, Tieck's subsequent
ventures in comedy, written with an increasing likelihood of influence by the Schlegels, are progressively further removed from
their concept of pure comedy. The Schlegels undoubtedly aroused
Tieck's interest in Aristophanes, but as Tieck lost the power to
experience and communicate a nonsensical mirth of his own, he
could only learn from the Athenian such mechanical tricks of the
trade as are displayed in *Anti-Faust*. And at the same time the
Schlegels may have been stimulating quite different interests to
which Tieck was more receptive.

Meanwhile, how were Tieck's fantastic farces received by the
Schlegels? On October 19, 1797, perhaps within a few days of
the first meeting between Tieck and Friedrich Schlegel in Berlin,
August Wilhelm wrote in Jena a review of *Der gestiefelte Kater*.[5]
Placing no credence in the alleged Italian source of the volume,
he still did not know the true identity of the "adapter," who
called himself Peter Leberecht.[6]

> The comic whimsy with which this . . . tale is dramatized does not stop
> at the boundaries of its subject matter. It plays in the actual world,
> right in our midst, and everything taking place in connection with the
> performance of the play . . . is brought upon the scene, so that one
> might term the whole . . . the play of a play. It is to be feared that the
> theorists will have quite a difficult time determining the category in
> which it really belongs. This much one can see . . . *it is a farce, a bold,
> mischievous farce*, in which the poet appears at every moment to inter-
> rupt himself and destroy his own work, only to shoot out so many more
> bits of raillery . . . in all directions like light darts. Yet this is done
> with such *gay good humor* that one could not help finding it delightful,
> even if our own cousins were to be made ludicrous. So whoever may have
> been brought into a too serious mood by the comedies presented in our
> theaters will find a good antidote in these follies.[7]

After describing some of the fun at the expense of theatrical
illusion, August Wilhelm concludes:

One sees there is quite a motley confusion; if only the author does not live to regret *having amused himself and others:* For—if we understand him correctly—he has *made fun of the* [theater-going] *public itself.* Now, it is well known that the *sacred populace of Athens* accepted fun poked at it from the stage with very good grace, but not all nations have the *gift of understanding jest* to the same degree. . . . Be that as it may; since the public cannot repay the compliment in person, let those do so upon whom Peter Leberecht has particularly declared war. But *let the weapons be jest,* for one cannot exorcise a demon of this sort by seriousness.[8]

Throughout the whole review, *Der gestiefelte Kater* and its mockery of the stage are seen as expressions of mischievous, jesting mirth and good-natured satire. Although the reviewer is reminded in the latter respect of the ancient Attic theater, he does not acclaim the play as a reincarnation of Aristophanic comedy. He takes it as an amusing *farce,* like that of Le Grand,[9] as one of those light, whimsical creations in which the modern theater recaptures something of the Aristophanic spirit. Finding only pure fun, an antidote against seriousness, August Wilhelm does not apply to *Der gestiefelte Kater* the concept of irony, which for him required an interplay of jest and earnest.

August Wilhelm's own expositions of the concepts of comedy and farce were written later than this review,[10] but we may assume that he had acquired thorough familiarity with his brother's ideas through oral discussion as well as from the essay on Greek comedy. The response which he received to the review in a letter from Friedrich, however, did not wholly share his enthusiasm: "The review of Tieck . . . delighted me greatly with its classic *grace* and urbanity, although I esteem Tieck much more for *Lovell* and as a person than for the *Kater,* which I do not find rich, insolent, or poetic enough. This last you have intimated also, if I understand you. He [Tieck] admits it too."[11]

This comment seems to have had its chastening effect upon August Wilhelm, for a few months later, when he again discusses *Der gestiefelte Kater* in a review of the *Volksmärchen von Peter Leberecht* for the *Athenäum,* his praise is noticeably tempered. He commends these tales, whose author he can now identify, to those who would "turn from a broad naturalism to more ethereal creations of fantasy, now conjuring up *cheerful jest,* now sounding the music of tender emotions." Such readers will find Tieck's style "very refreshing" even though "not yet fully

developed." *Der gestiefelte Kater* has aroused greater public
notice than Tieck's other tales because of its strikingly uncon-
ventional satiric technique: "To bring the German theater, and
all that goes with it, bodily onto the stage in a story from Mother
Goose is indeed unheard of. Were the satire methodical, declama-
tory, venomous—but quite the opposite, it is altogether mischievous and farcical, in short, contrary to all order. I give up the
author for lost; he will never recover from the blows he has
dealt . . . ," will never gain forgiveness for the "rash lightness"
with which these "bits of roguishness" have burst upon the
world.[12]

The laudatory effect of such ironic reprimands is offset, however, by a concluding recommendation—to be sure, without
special reference to any one of the *Volksmärchen*—that their
author learn from "his friend Shakespeare" the importance of
concentrating his art upon one focus so that it will not "come
tardy off," that he "gather himself together" and select those
outward forms which of themselves compel concentration.[13] In
the light of this most appropriate advice, it seems puzzling that
in the same review August Wilhelm calls *Blaubart* the most
mature dramatic piece in the collection.[14] If maturity has anything to do with the desired concentration, how could the ram-
bling tragicomedy with its myriad serious and farcical characters and subplots be preferred over a short comedy which consistently aims to evoke mirth through nonsense? A possible
answer is that August Wilhelm was not thinking of concentration
within a given play upon a single kind of poetic evocation but
rather would suggest that Tieck concentrate all his dramatic
talents upon one Shakespearean category, the ironic,[15] seriocomic
romantic drama.

There is reason to believe that a similar preference also motivated Friedrich Schlegel's criticism that *Der gestiefelte Kater*
was "not rich, insolent, or poetic enough." At first sight this
might appear to be nothing other than an apt comparison with
Aristophanic comedy, and in the case of the second adjective,
frech, Friedrich was no doubt thinking of the rough, daring personal satire and saline jest which we miss in Tieck's farce. But
his other utterances of this period make it appear unlikely that
he had in mind precisely the richness and poetic quality of Aristophanes. Friedrich's very next letter to August Wilhelm reveals

a preference for the narrative *Volksmärchen* over the dramatized ones.[16] But *Die schöne Magelone, Der blonde Eckbert,* and *Die Heymonskinder,* which make up the bulk of the prose tales, are distinguished by moods of nostalgic mysticism or ineffable horror, by a sentimentally idealized medieval atmosphere, by the sympathy of flowers and birds with the emotions of the characters, and by the profuse interspersion of ingratiating but shallow lyrics like the famous "Waldeinsamkeit." It would thus seem possible that the variety of moods and of prose and verse forms to be found in these tales impressed Friedrich Schlegel at this time as *richness,* that he considered their nostalgia and their epic-lyric-musical synestheticism *poetic,* and that these were the qualities which he missed in *Der gestiefelte Kater.* This interpretation gains further support from the 418th *Athenäum-Fragment,* which compares the novels *William Lovell* and *Franz Sternbalds Wanderungen* with "the *poetic* arabesques which [Tieck] formed out of old tales," praising the "fantastic *fullness,*" "sense for irony," and "especially the deliberate *variety* and unity of coloring."[17] The novel *Sternbald,* with its nostalgia for the age of Dürer and for the free and aimless wanderings of young artists through romantic landscapes, accompanied by that same repeated transition to a facile lyricism which one finds in the prose *Volksmärchen,* is indeed Friedrich Schlegel's favorite among Tieck's works. He recommends it to his brother as "the first novel since Cervantes that is romantic, and in addition, far superior to [Goethe's] *Meister.*"[18]

Another letter, dating from the same winter (1797-98) as the comments on *Der gestiefelte Kater* and Tieck's other fairy tales, speaks warmly of a new work, really "a continuation of the *Volksmärchen,*" for which Tieck is seeking a publisher. The date makes it virtually certain that Walzel, the editor of this correspondence, is correct in identifying the work in question with *Prinz Zerbino.* "Besides what you will say . . . about individual merits, you can also promise yourself *upon my word* (the more so, because he has told me very much of his plans, and even read a sample) the *greatest heterogeneity.* If you have already read the *Volksmärchen* and *Lovell,* my reminder is superfluous."[19]

All these utterances are symptomatic of a profound change in the general standards of Friedrich Schlegel's criticism—and consequently also in his estimate of comedy—since the essay on

Aristophanes. What he now valued in all kinds of poetic creation was a synthesis of the heterogeneous, a merging of narrative, lyric, and dramatic forms, an imitation of pictorial and musical effects, and a romantic nostalgia expressed with subtle irony, precisely the characteristics which he could find in *Franz Stern-balds Wanderungen*, the narrative *Volksmärchen*, and the embryonic *Zerbino*. His poetic ideal was a novel—or a drama with the "air of a novel"—which would present "a compendium, an encyclopedia of the whole spiritual life of an individual of genius,"[20] an ideal which found its most famous definition in the 116th *Athenäum-Fragment*:

> Romantic poetry is a progressive universal poetry. It is not only destined to reunite all separate categories of poetry . . . It is also its intention and mission, now to mix, now to fuse, poetry and prose, genius and criticism, artistic poetry and natural poetry, . . . to fill and saturate the forms of art with concentrated cultural material of every kind, and to animate them with the pulsations of humor. . . . The romantic style of poetry is the only one which is more than a style and is, so to speak, identical with poetic art itself; for, in a certain sense, all poetry is or should be romantic.[21]

To the Friedrich Schlegel of the late 1790's, no poetic work could seem of great significance unless it embodied the kind of universality that meant diversity. The nonsensical merriment of fantastic comedy might be a welcome ingredient in such universal poetry, but any work which was focused entirely upon this single poetic experience could be of no great account. It might amuse and serve a useful satiric purpose, but it could not be *rich* or *poetic* enough to provide a rallying point for the critical revolution which the Schlegels intended to touch off with the *Athenäum*. These principles, imparted to August Wilhelm during the winter of 1797-98, in which the brothers were preparing their new journal, together with Friedrich's gentle admonition for the uncritical acclaim of the first review, induced August Wilhelm to lower his estimate of *Der gestiefelte Kater* in the second one.

Nevertheless, there are other utterances to show that Friedrich's reaction to *Der gestiefelte Kater* was not wholly negative, that he did find it amusing, and thoroughly approved both its satiric direction and its comic treatment of the stage. Otherwise he would not have honored Tieck's farce with a *Fragment* in the *Athenäum* (Number 307): "When I pronounce my antipathy to the feline species, I make an exception of Peter Leberecht's Puss in Boots. He does indeed have claws, and whoever is scratched by them may well cry out against him. Others, however, can be amused by the way in which he strolls about, so to speak, upon the roof of dramatic art."[22] Additional favorable comments, contained in letters written to August Wilhelm during the spring of 1798, are an expression of surprise that the noted philologist F. A. Wolf, in view of his "limited . . . sense for poetry," could be pleased with the *Kater*,[23] and Friedrich's agreement with the more tempered approval of the play in August Wilhelm's review of the *Volksmärchen:* "What you have written about Tieck pleases me exceptionally well. The viewpoint is very clearly defined, and I don't find it too much."[24]

One may, then, distinguish two reactions of the Schlegels to Tieck's farcical comedy, both traceable to esthetic concepts originating with Friedrich: The unqualified praise of August Wilhelm's first review is an application of the comic standards enunciated in Friedrich's essay of 1794; the mixed reception accorded in August Wilhelm's second review and the brief comments of Friedrich himself stem from the latter's new demand for the comprehensive experience, heterogeneous content, and synesthetic form of "universal poetry."

These two discrepant reactions reflect the incompatibility of Friedrich's earlier concept of "pure comedy" with the doctrine of romantic "universality" which he now espoused. We have seen in an earlier chapter that he gradually became conscious of this incompatibility himself and finally accepted the consequences, renouncing the pure ancient comedy in favor of that mixed *romantic comedy* which he found in Shakespeare and Calderón. August Wilhelm Schlegel, to be sure, tried to maintain the two ideals side by side, so as to champion both against the different, and allegedly nonpoetic, seriocomic mixture exhibited by middle-class comedy. Nevertheless, the over-all tendency of his critical writings, and doubtless that of his personal conversation, would encourage contemporary writers to emulate the diversity of romantic rather than the unity of ancient drama. It is, then, not surprising that Tieck's own attempt to create a romantic comedy was warmly recommended by Friedrich Schlegel early in 1802 to the publisher Reimer: "It is called *Octavianus*, an old romantic history, a comedy, but entirely in the higher sense of the word . . ."[25] Many years later, in 1827, August Wilhelm added his endorsement of *Octavianus,* by listing it among a small number of Tieck's "more mature works," which could not adequately be appraised without probing "the innermost secrets of poetry."[26]

The relevance of the Schlegels' conception of Aristophanic comedy to *Der gestiefelte Kater* is corroborated by August Wilhelm's two reviews, even when we allow for the reservations in the second one conditioned by the new trend of Friedrich Schlegel's esthetic predilections. There is, on the other hand, nothing in the writings of either Schlegel to justify the traditional critical approach to Tieck's fantastic comedy from the criterion of irony. In this respect, the most that Friedrich Schlegel ever credits to Tieck is the "sense for irony" noted by the 418th *Athenäum-Fragment* in *Franz Sternbalds Wanderungen* and in the "poetic arabesques formed out of old tales."[27] Once one examines this *Fragment* as a whole, it appears extremely unlikely that Schlegel was thinking of *Der gestiefelte Kater* except as part of a larger unit, the *Volksmärchen,* and certain that he was not concerned with the outright destruction of illusion. The *Fragment* is primarily a comparison of the two novels, *Lovell* and *Sternbald*—the only other work explicitly named being the *Herzensergiessungen eines kunstliebenden Klosterbruders,* the collection of reverently enthusiastic anecdotes about Renaissance artists on which Tieck collaborated with Wackenroder. The three identified works are all in the narrative form, essentially serious, and untainted by infractions of representative illusion. *Lovell* is praised for the profound, thorough, and interesting portrayal of an entirely new kind of character in its "poetic" hero, but the novel as a whole is found to be "a conflict of prose and poetry" and to fluctuate "between instinct and design because it does not have enough of either." *Sternbald* and the "poetic arabesques," on the other hand, demonstrate an ironic sense by combining fullness and lightness, unity and variety; and in these more mature creations "the romantic spirit appears to muse over itself in pleasing fantasy." Here Schlegel is thinking of the delicate parody—through subtle but deliberate exaggeration—of the author's own romantic nostalgia for a visionary poetic existence, which we find in *Sternbald* and in some of those narrative *Volksmärchen* preferred by Schlegel over *Der gestiefelte Kater.*[28] The similarity of these merits to the ironic qualities which the latter attributed to Cervantes, Shakespeare, and Boccaccio is unmistakable.[29]

After examining the question of the Schlegels' positive contribution to Tieck's comic creation and the reception which they accorded it, we should now consider the possibility that they influenced Tieck's concentration upon comedy in a negative sense, that they helped him to *unlearn* the art of fantastic farcical comedy, which he had best displayed before his first contacts with them. We cannot overlook the emergence of a tendency to sacrifice nonsensical mirth to a fusion of heterogeneous moods, styles, characters, and situations in the comedies written during Tieck's early association with the Schlegels, *Die verkehrte Welt* and *Prinz Zerbino,* or the culmination of this tendency in *Kaiser Octavianus,* conceived during the association's most intimate phase. Tieck himself tells us (in his essay on Falk, Merkel, and Beck) that by the year 1800 he had already cast off the "serene, unclouded whimsy" and "lightheartedness" of his early fantastic comedies in favor of a more serious outlook, and it may be significant that he refers in the same passage to his friendship with Friedrich and August Wilhelm Schlegel.[30] Of course, this new development was rooted in Tieck's own spontaneous inclinations, but there is evidence that the Schlegels did much to encourage it. Friedrich's dictum that *Der gestiefelte Kater* was not "rich, insolent, or poetic enough" had been confirmed by the author's own admission,[31] undoubtedly expressed during conversations in which the critic pointed out these weaknesses and thereby suggested the principles to be followed in future creation. The next few years, which Tieck spent in unbroken association with one or both of the Schlegels, offered him abundant opportunity to learn from their lips and from their pronouncements in the *Athenäum* the cardinal importance of "universality," "heterogeneity," and "fullness." And when the same respected mentor who had found *Der gestiefelte Kater* "not rich enough" expressed his delight at the "heterogeneity" of *Prinz Zerbino,* Tieck must have been encouraged to penetrate even more deeply into the lush Garden of *Universal* Poetry.

However, there is more than such plausible inferences to confirm the direction of the Schlegels' influence upon Tieck's dramatic writing. We have already seen, in August Wilhelm's review of the *Volksmärchen,* the hint that their author would profit by a more concentrated emulation of Shakespearean romantic drama. A letter written by August Wilhelm to Tieck, contemporaneously with this review and with Friedrich's acclamation of *Zerbino,* is more explicit. August Wilhelm expresses surprise at the scant evidence of Tieck's familiarity with Shakespeare which he encounters in the *Volksmärchen* and suggests: "Perhaps this is only because you have not yet dramatized anything in Shakespeare's form. A romantic-comic drama, the serious part in iambic pentameter, which might well be interspersed with rhymes, only the comic dialogue in prose, would certainly win you splendid success."[32] Some three years after receiving this advice, Tieck began work on *Octavianus,* which, as he later conceded to Solger, would never have been written but for his "perhaps exaggerated admiration" of Shakespeare's *Pericles.*[33] Only one more ingredient was needed to provide the complete recipe, both for *Octavianus* and for *romantic comedy* in general, that Spanish sauce to which the Schlegels and Tieck alike had meanwhile become addicted. Its incorporation is acknowledged in the prefatory comment on *Kaiser Octavianus* in Tieck's *Schriften:* ". . . there had been so much talk in Germany of the character of the romantic; inspired by Calderón with enthusiasm for allegorical poetry, I attempted in this strange tale to set down in allegorical, lyric, and dramatic form my conception of romantic poetry."[34] We know that the talk about the romantic and the drawing of inspiration from Calderón at the turn of the century originated with Friedrich and August Wilhelm Schlegel.

Tieck's natural disposition toward a diffuse and conglomerate poetic style had been only briefly interrupted by the exhilarated mirth which gave birth to *Der gestiefelte Kater.* He probably could not have duplicated the relative concentration and uniformity of mood displayed in this single farce in any case; but the notions of romantic universality, heterogeneity, and synestheticism which he imbibed from the Schlegels between 1797 and 1802 discouraged him from trying. The "musical" interludes and idyllic scenes of *Die verkehrte Welt* probably already reflect the new esthetics of Friedrich Schlegel, and without doubt the latter's approval of the disunity in Tieck's outline of *Zerbino* aggravated this defect in the completed work. August Wilhelm Schlegel urged Tieck to emulate the seriocomic, epic-lyric-dramatic qualities in romantic dramas like the semi-Shakespearean

Pericles, and Tieck followed the advice in *Kaiser Octavianus.*
The comic talents which in 1797 had chanced to exemplify the
esthetic values discovered by Friedrich Schlegel in the Old Attic
Comedy were, by 1802, turned to a calculated embodiment of the
new and incompatible poetic ideals of the *Athenäum.*

CONCLUSION

With *Der gestiefelte Kater,* Tieck introduced a fantastic-farcical comedy designed to arouse sustained laughter through a variety of glaring incongruities, most of them irrational or physically impossible, some involving the gross exaggeration or distortion of familiar experience. This play was intended for the stage, and a conspicuous part of its jest deals with the theater itself. Its foremost objective is to transport the spectator—or the reader who imagines himself a spectator—into a state of exuberant mirth. The author has his satiric motives as well, but these, too, are sublimated in merriment, so that satire may only appear as a vehicle for comedy. The playful nonsense of Tieck's farce precludes the systematic development of dramatic suspense and deliberately contradicts the underlying assumptions of theatrical representation, but the comic effects remain theatrical in their dependence upon an actual or vividly imagined stage. This farce is virtually devoid of structural form but derives a kind of unity from its consistently jesting tone. Throughout most of a second comedy, *Die verkehrte Welt,* Tieck pursues the same objective, but he frequently becomes lost in satire that has ceased to be comical, in lyricism and pastoral idyll, and in conceits of verbal "music."

The farcical comedy which Tieck sought to create in these two plays exhibits striking parallels with the notion of a "pure" fantastic comedy abstracted by Friedrich and August Wilhelm Schlegel from the work of Aristophanes. As a critical appraisal of the latter's actual comic creation, their theory is unbalanced and inadequate, glossing over his earnest polemics and overlooking some of the deepest sources of his poetic greatness and universality, but it is the first attempt of European criticism to evaluate Aristophanic drama *as comedy* and to establish the esthetic legitimacy of fantastic comedy in general.

Although there actually is a relationship between the comic objectives and techniques of Tieck and Aristophanes, the achievement of even Tieck's best fantastic farce, *Der gestiefelte Kater,* falls immeasurably short of Attic comedy. Tieck lacked the Greek poet's wealth of comic resources, the vigor and brisk pace of his jest, and he could not infuse true universality into his work. The limitations of Tieck's comic artistry are particularly manifest in his one-sided development of a single one of the countless motifs exploited by Aristophanes, the incongruity of theatrical representation. Here the fault lies, not in Tieck's drastic employment, but in his monotonous repetition and elaboration of the device. In addition to the vast difference in their achievement, there is also a difference in the temper of the mirth which each poet sought to evoke: with the Athenian, the ribald laughter of lusty, pugnacious manhood, with the German, the harmless play of childlike whimsy. Unfortunately, Tieck at times mars this impression in *Der gestiefelte Kater* with bookish pedantry, and in *Die verkehrte Welt* he smothers his jesting fantasy under a mass of intellectual gymnastics and lifeless verbiage.

Tieck's subsequent comedies incorporate practically all the fantastic-comic devices of these two and add others directly borrowed from Attic comedy, but they never recapture the hilarity imparted throughout much of *Der gestiefelte Kater*. At best, as in the case of *Das Ungeheuer und der verzauberte Wald* and *Rotkäppchen*, they achieve limited success in quite different modifications of fantastic comedy; at worst, as in *Prinz Zerbino*, all track of a unifying esthetic objective is lost. Most of Tieck's later experiments with the dramatic form are written solely for readers and forego the vitality of reference to the stage. The most ambitious of all his ventures in comedy, *Kaiser Octavianus*, is strictly a closet drama, draws most of its comic effects from realistic sources, and, as a studied exercise in what the Romanticists themselves understood by *romantic comedy*, it exemplifies a phase of their theory distinct from the concept of pure, fantastic jest.

The resemblance between *Der gestiefelte Kater* and the Schlegels' interpretation of Aristophanes was almost certainly coincidental. By the time their friendship with Tieck began, his own capacity to create fantastic comedy was declining, and their interest in a uniform expression of mirth was giving way to preoccupation with romantic comedy or drama and "universal poetry." Friedrich Schlegel soon afterwards repudiated the ideal of pure comedy, and August Wilhelm's attempt to co-ordinate it with seriocomic romantic comedy in a single system of dramatic theory is forced and unconvincing. Any significant influence which the two brothers exerted upon Tieck was directed away from the sustained jesting nonsense of *Der gestiefelte Kater* toward the interplay of realistic comedy and nostalgic pathos exemplified by *Kaiser Octavianus*. The changing interests of the Schlegels also explain their tepid approval of *Der gestiefelte Kater* after the hearty acclaim with which August Wilhelm had first greeted it.

Tieck contributed to German literature one readable and not altogether unactable fantastic farce with the single brilliant comic characterization of its titular hero, but this and Tieck's other creative efforts in the same direction, together with the critical studies of the Schlegels, rendered their most important service in the intense and lasting interest which they aroused in the comic genius of Aristophanes. Literary historians have generally obscured these contributions by taking the satire of *Der gestiefelte Kater* as an end in itself, by treating the play as the most extreme illustration of the tenets of German Romanticism, and by confusing the farcical exploitation of theatrical portrayal with Friedrich Schlegel's concept of irony. Tieck's satire is, in this instance at least, a vehicle for jest. Neither the comedy itself, nor the theory of the Schlegels which it happens to exemplify, represents the full efflorescence of German Romantic tendencies. The theory of a pure fantastic comedy belonged to the classical phase of Friedrich Schlegel's criticism, in which it still set a premium on artistic unity, and its creation resulted from a fortuitous state of mind momentarily enjoyed by Tieck on the threshold of his own Romanticism. The exaltation of irrationality and playful fantasy, license and caprice, the disregard for structural integration and representative illusion— these are indeed typical of German Romanticism; but the cardinal tenet of Friedrich Schlegel's school, that poetry must strive to express an infinite heterogeneity of experience through an inexhaustible variety of artistic means, is violated by a work devoted wholly to the evocation of mirth through nonsense. Fantastic comedy sprang from Romantic roots, but it was quickly choked out by the rank foliage shooting up around it in the Romantic Garden of Poesy, and neither Tieck nor his younger imitators ever succeeded in grafting it onto the exotic growth of *Universalpoesie*.

In destroying the representative illusion of the stage, Tieck has been charged with the grossest of all Romantic offenses against poetic unity. Yet Aristophanes had long since demonstrated that this device can be an effective implement of fantastic farce. Tieck relied much too heavily on this single resource, but even so *Der gestiefelte Kater* is less guilty of disunity or of frustrating its own purposes than many another literary product of German Romanticism.

The failure of critics to recognize Tieck's comic objectives has led them to appraise *Der gestiefelte Kater* by the inappropriate measuring rod of Friedrich Schlegel's irony. Tieck's *farce* is not to be evaluated by its success in expressing Friedrich Schlegel's ironic philosophy of life and literature, nor does it afford a useful illustration of the latter. The fantastic play of nonsensical jest and the urbane ironic smile are reactions to the same fundamental situation in which the Romanticist finds himself, but they are *different* reactions. As a French critic has said, "The Romanticist is above all a seeker of the Absolute. . . . The Romanticist neither knows how nor is able to wait: he believes that the Absolute is at hand's length and can be plucked in a single gesture . . ." The hard lesson that the Absolute can never be securely grasped, that "the majesty of the ineffable and the poverty of its messengers" are never to be separated, "is what the Romanticists called Irony."[1] The same critic holds the ironic smile to be "the sole effective defense against despair."[2] But some Romanticists found another defense against, or more precisely a release from, their despair in the wanton play of intoxicated comic fantasy. We encounter it outside of Germany in two of Romanticism's most uncompromising seekers after the Absolute: Musset's unceasingly frustrated quest for the Absolute in erotic love renews its strength through the dancing wit symbolized by his jester Fantasio. Shelley sustains his unattainable Promethean visions with the release provided by mischievous boyish pranks. Mary Shelley's justification of these reads almost like a translation from Tieck's *Phantasus*: "He was playful and indulged in the wild spirit that mocked itself and others—not in bitterness, but in sport."[3] It is as a manifestation of this wild spirit of playful mockery that we should judge the merits of *Der gestiefelte Kater*.

NOTES

NOTES FOR INTRODUCTION

[1] The inner quotation is from the 307th *Athenäum-Fragment*, which will be examined in ch. vi. Neither here nor elsewhere does Schlegel suggest that Hinze may symbolize *irony*.

[2] "An willkürlichster Behandlung der Objektenwelt, an Phantastik und Ironie, an Selbstparodie und Hinwegsetzen über die prosaischen Gesetze der Wirklichkeit fehlte es dem Tieckschen Märchen- und Komödienhumor wahrlich nicht. Sehr füglich daher konnte Schlegel den Berliner Dichter zur Illustration seiner ästhetischen Doktrin verwerten. Der 'auf dem Dache der dramatischen Kunst herumspazierende' Kater Hinze war nahezu ein Symbol der Ironie." Rudolf Haym, *Die romantische Schule*, 4th ed. (Berlin, 1920), p. 303.

[3] I find no instance of this phrase in Friedrich Schlegel's own writings.

[4] Hermann Hettner, *Die romantische Schule in ihrem inneren Zusammenhange mit Goethe und Schiller* (Braunschweig, 1850), p. 63.

[5] See *Johann Elias Schlegels aesthetische und dramaturgische Schriften*, ed. Johann von Antoniewicz, Deutsche Litteraturdenkmale des 18. und 19. Jahrhunderts, XXVI (Heilbronn, 1887), pp. 132 ff. Cf. Elizabeth M. Wilkinson, *Johann Elias Schlegel* (Oxford, 1945), pp. 76 ff.

[6] The *Hamburgische Dramaturgie* (42. Stück) excludes from tragedy anything that might remind the spectators of the means by which illusion is produced, such as the mere mention of a theater, but concedes that the laughter of comedy can take illusion less strictly than the sympathy of tragedy.

[7] The concept of illusion is foreign to Aristotle's *Poetics* but is sometimes associated in modern esthetics with the Aristotelian principle of delight evoked by artful imitation. This is one kind of illusion which Tieck himself recognizes (see ch. v, below, p. 92).

[8] Notably by H. Günther, *Romantische Kritik und Satire bei Ludwig Tieck* (diss. Leipzig, 1907).

NOTES FOR CHAPTER ONE

[1] Alfred E. Lussky, *Tieck's Romantic Irony* (Chapel Hill, 1932), pp. 1-44.

[2] "The Subjectivity or Objectivity of Friedrich Schlegel's Poetic Irony," *Germanic Review*, XXVI (1951), 173-191. This article will hereafter be cited as "Schlegel's Poetic Irony."

[3] "Methode? Ironie bei Fr. Schlegel und bei Solger," *Helicon*, I (1938), 33-50. This article will hereafter be cited as "Methode?"

[4] Hettner, *Die romantische Schule in ihrem inneren Zusammenhange mit Goethe und Schiller*, pp. 63 ff.

[5] *Ibid.*, p. 9.

[6] *Ibid.*, pp. 63, 66 ff. The longer passage is translated from pp. 69 f.

[7] *Ibid.*, pp. 68 f.

[8] Haym, *Die romantische Schule*, pp. 95 ff.

[9] *Ibid.*, pp. 99 ff. The passage translated is from p. 100.

[10] *Ibid.*, pp. 295-303.

[11] Friedrich Schlegel, *Seine prosaischen Jugendschriften*, ed. J. Minor (Wien, 1882), II, 242, 244. This edition will hereafter be cited as Minor. Cf. Marie Joachimi[-Dege], *Die Weltanschauung der deutschen Romantik* (Jena and Leipzig, 1905), pp. 176 f., footnote; also "Schlegel's Poetic Irony," pp. 180 ff.

[12] See "Schlegel's Poetic Irony," pp. 184 f.

[13] Ricarda Huch, *Die Romantik* (Tübingen and Stuttgart, 1951), pp. 253 ff., quotation from p. 255.

[14] *Ibid.*, pp. 258 f.

[15] See "Schlegel's Poetic Irony," pp. 182-9.

[16] *Op. cit.*, pp. 262 f.

[17] *Ibid.*, pp. 283 f., 293.

[18] Anna Tumarkin, *Die romantische Weltanschauung* (Bern, 1920), p. 102.

[19] Minor, II, 296.

[20] Tumarkin, *op. cit.*, pp. 70 ff., 102, 105 f.

[21] "Friedrich Schlegel," in *Romantiker* (Berlin-Wilmersdorf, 1930), pp. 13 ff.

[22] "Ludwig Tieck," in *Romantiker: Neue Folge* (Berlin-Wilmersdorf, 1931), p. 94.

[23] *Ibid.*, p. 99.

[24] *Ibid.*, pp. 103 f.

[25] *Ibid.*, pp. 94 ff.

[26] "Jener muthwillige Wahnsinn, der oft die selbst erfundenen Gesetze wieder vernichtet." Ludwig Tieck, *Schriften*, VI (Berlin, 1828), xx. Cf. also the statement of the "Playwright" in *Der gestiefelte Kater*, quoted on p. 60, and other passages quoted in ch. v.

[27] *Die Weltanschauung der deutschen Romantik*, p. 167, and *Deutsche Shakespeare-Probleme im XVIII. Jahrhundert und im Zeitalter der Romantik*, Untersuchungen zur neueren Sprach- und Literaturgeschichte, XII (Leipzig, 1907), pp. 165 f. These works will hereafter be cited as *Weltanschauung* and *Probleme*.

[28] *Weltanschauung*, p. 174.

[29] In the 51st *Athenäum-Fragment*, Minor, II, 211.

[30] See "Schlegel's Poetic Irony," pp. 178 f.

[31] *Weltanschauung*, pp. 175 f.; italics represent the author's spaced type.

[32] Minor, II, 361 f. Schlegel attributes this alternation of irony and enthusiasm jointly to Shakespeare and Cervantes; yet Frau Joachimi-Dege refuses to recognize anyone but Shakespeare as an exemplar of Schlegel's irony. See *Probleme*, p. 167.

[33] *Probleme*, pp. 169 ff., *Weltanschauung*, pp. 184 ff.

[34] Seventh *Lyceum-Fragment*, Minor, II, 184.

[35] Sixty-sixth *Lyceum-Fragment*, Minor, II, 192.

[36] *Weltanschauung*, pp. 184 f. The passage in question, the 418th *Athenäum-Fragment*, is discussed in ch. vi.

[37] Robert M. Wernaer, *Romanticism and the Romantic School in Germany* (New York and London, 1910), pp. 185, 188.

[38] *Ibid.*, pp. 196 ff., quotation from p. 198.

[39] *Ibid.*, pp. 200 ff.

[40] Walter Silz, *Early German Romanticism: Its Founders and Heinrich von Kleist* (Cambridge, Mass., 1929), pp. 180 f.

[41] *Ibid.*, pp. 182 f., quotation from p. 183.

[42] *Ibid.*, p. 178.

[43] Lussky, *op. cit.*, pp. 45 ff., 53 f., 57 ff.

[44] *Ibid.*, pp. 80 f.

[45] *Ibid.*, pp. 92 ff.

[46] He cites "examples of the sheerest destruction of the literary objectivity" of *Wilhelm Meister* (*ibid.*, p. 99) in Goethe's use of the first personal pronoun and his mention of the novel while narrating it. The present investigator does not believe that such devices, which are, after all, traditional narrative conventions, impair the kind of "illusion" we expect of a storyteller. Goethe does not follow Sterne in devoting substantial portions of his novel to the discussion of its genesis, nor do his *characters*, as in *Don Quixote*, speak of their own novel. The attitude expressed by Goethe toward his hero is patronizing and gently ironic, but it is not the contempt or ridicule found by Professor Lussky (pp. 103 ff.).

[47] *Ibid.*, pp. 96 ff., 108 ff.

[48] *Ibid.*, pp. 114 f., 118 ff.

[49] *Ibid.*, p. 115.

[50] *Ibid.*, p. 118.

[51] *Ibid.*, p. 117.

[52] *Ibid.*, pp. 159-233.

[53] See his remark to Köpke quoted in ch. v, below, p. 100.

[54] *Op. cit.*, p. 241; Lussky's italics.

[55] *Ibid.*, p. 242.

[56] *Ibid.*, p. 196.

[57] Schlegel attributes "Sinn für Ironie" to the latter novel in the 418th *Athenäum-Fragment*, when he compares it with *William Lovell;* see note 36, above.

[58] *August Wilhelm und Friedrich Schlegel*, ed. Oskar F. Walzel, Deutsche National-Litteratur, CXLIII (Stuttgart, [1891-92]), pp. xxxv f. The passage translated is from p. xxxv.

[59] "Im frühromantischen Kreise erstehen Schöpfungen voll romantischer Ironie, ehe Fr. Schlegel die Lehre von der Ironie weiter ausgeführt und zu einem Grundsatz der Schule gemacht hatte. . . . Tieck spendet . . . Belege der romantischen Theorie, die den Theoretikern ausgezeichnet taugten, von ihnen aber nicht angeregt worden waren. . . .

"Die einleuchtendste, nächstliegende und von der Romantik am ausgiebigsten genutzte Form der romantischen Ironie ist die Zerstörung der dramatischen Illusion. Fr. Schlegels Definitionen der romantischen Ironie . . . liessen sich diesen Zug nicht entgehen, wenn sie auf 'die mimische Manier eines gewöhnlichen guten italienischen Buffo' . . . sich bezogen. . . .

"Der 'Gestiefelte Kater' übertrumpft alles, was bis dahin auf der Bühne geschehen war, um die Bühnentäuschung mutwillig zu zerstören und allen Vereinbarungen, die zwischen der Bühne und ihren Zuschauern zu bestehen pflegen, übermütig ein Bein zu stellen." Oskar Walzel, *Deutsche Romantik: II. Die Dichtung* (5th ed.; Leipzig and Berlin, 1926), pp. 54 f.

[60] Walzel, *Romantisches*, Mnemosyne, XVIII (Bonn, 1934), p. 76.

[61] The 116th and 238th *Athenäum-Fragmente*, Minor, II, 220, 242.

[62] Walzel, *Vom Geistesleben des 18. und 19. Jahrhunderts* (Leipzig, 1911), pp. 89 ff.

[63] *Ibid.*, pp. 90 ff.; *Romantisches*, pp. 48 ff.

[64] *Deutsche Romantik*, II, 55.

[65] *Romantisches*, p. 73; cf. also the similar statement on p. 64.

[66] "Es giebt alte und moderne Gedichte, die durchgängig im Ganzen und überall den göttlichen Hauch der Ironie athmen. Es lebt in ihnen eine wirklich transcendentale Buffonerie. Im Innern, die Stimmung, welche alles übersieht und sich über alles Bedingte unendlich erhebt, auch über eigne Kunst, Tugend, oder Genialität: im Äussern, in der Ausführung die mimische Manier eines gewöhnlichen guten italiänischen Buffo." Minor, II, 188 f.; the portion quoted here is on p. 189.

[67] Here Walzel is quoting from the 108th *Lyceum-Fragment*, Minor, II, 198.

[68] "Der Schluss des Fragments mag veranlasst haben, dass Störung der Illusion vor anderem als eigentliche Auswirkung der romantischen Ironie angesehen wurde und wird. Darsteller romantischer Dichtung verharrten gern bei diesem Einzelfall, auch weil sie . . . ihren Lesern etwas recht Handgreifliches bieten wollten. (Ich selbst möchte nicht von fern den Anschein wecken, ich hätte es immer besser gemacht.) Die Folge war, dass man in romantischer Ironie nur Rechtfertigung der Illusionsstörung, in Illusionsstörung die eigentliche Leistung romantischer Ironie sah . . . Gegen solche Missdeutung kann gar nicht genug der 'unauflösliche Widerstreit des Unbedingten und des Bedingten' aufgeboten werden, dann die Stimmung, die sich über alles Bedingte unendlich erhebt." "Methode?," p. 42.

[69] Schlegel's term *Gedichte* signifies literary creations in prose as well as in verse. The *Deutsches Wörterbuch* attests that this was common usage in the latter part of the eighteenth century. In his essay on Goethe's *Wilhelm Meister*, Schlegel directly applies the term *Gedicht* to that novel (Minor, II, 177), which is undoubtedly one of the *neue Gedichte* he has in mind in the 42nd *Lyceum-Fragment*. Regarding the *alte Gedichte*, which he nowhere explicitly identifies, see "Schlegel's Poetic Irony," pp. 188 f.

[70] See above, p. 12.

[71] Minor, II, 175.

[72] "Man lasse sich also dadurch, dass der Dichter selbst die Personen und die Begebenheiten so leicht und so launig zu nehmen, den Helden fast nie ohne Ironie zu erwähnen, und auf sein Meisterwerk selbst von der Höhe seines Geistes herabzulächeln scheint, nicht täuschen, als sey es ihm nicht der heiligste Ernst." *Ibid.*, p. 171.

[73] "Es ist . . . eine gewisse zierliche Albernheit . . . Und dennoch unterhält uns das närrische Wesen, ja eben diese ironische Unbedeutendheit macht den eigentlichen Reiz davon, wie die innere Schalkheit bei dem sittsamen Ton der bis zum Pomphaften edelmüthigen Reden." *Ibid.*, p. 399.

NOTES FOR CHAPTER TWO

[1] Minor, I, 11-20.

[2] *Ibid.*, p. 11.

[3] See Carl Enders, *Friedrich Schlegel* (Leipzig, 1913), pp. 24, 201-253, *et passim*.

[4] Minor, I, 11 ff. The quotation (p. 13) reads: "Eine Person . . . , die sich bloss durch ihren eignen Willen bestimmt, und die es offenbar macht dass sie weder innern noch äussern Schranken unterworfen ist, stellt die vollkommne innre und äussre persönliche Freiheit dar. Dadurch dass sie im frohen Genusse ihrer Selbst nur aus reiner Willkür und Laune handelt, absichtlich ohne Grund oder wider Gründe, wird die innre Freiheit sichtbar; die äussre in dem Muthwillen, mit dem sie äussre Schranken verletzt, während das Gesetz grossmüthig seinem Rechte entsagt."

[5] *Ibid.*, pp. 13 f. The quotation (p. 14) reads: "Wenn irgend etwas in menschlichen Werken göttlich genannt werden darf, so ist es die schöne Fröhlichkeit und die erhabne Freiheit in den Werken des *Aristophanes*."

[6] *Ibid.*, pp. 14 ff.

[7] "Die Satire des Aristophanes ist sehr oft nicht poetisch sondern persönlich, und eben so demagogisch als die Art mit der er den Wünschen und den Meinungen des Volkes schmeichelt." *Ibid.*, p. 17.

[8] "Diese Verletzung ist nicht Ungeschicklichkeit, sondern besonnener Muthwille, überschäumende Lebensfülle, und thut oft gar keine üble Wir-

kung, erhöht sie vielmehr, denn vernichten kann sie die Täuschung doch nicht. Die höchste Regsamkeit des Lebens muss wirken, muss zerstören; findet sie nichts ausser sich, so wendet sie sich zurück auf einen geliebten Gegenstand, auf sich selbst, ihr eigen Werk; sie verletzt dann, um zu reizen, ohne zu zerstören." *Ibid.*, p. 18.

[9] *Ibid.*, pp. 18 f. The quotation, on p. 19, reads as follows: "Sie erzeugt einen Rausch des Lebens welcher den Geist mit sich fortreisst; und Schönheiten welche die Selbstthätigkeit zu sehr in Anspruch nehmen, gehen verloren. Die vollkommne Kausalverknüpfung, die innere dramatische Nothwendigkeit und Vollständigkeit, sind viel zu schwerfällig für einen leichten zerstreuenden Rausch. . . ."

[10] *Romantisches*, pp. 63 f.

[11] See *Ueber naive und sentimentalische Dichtung*, in *Schillers Sämtliche Werke, Säkular-Ausgabe*, ed. E. von der Hellen (Stuttgart and Berlin [1904-5]), XII, 196 ff.

[12] Minor, I, 18 f.

[13] *Ibid.*, pp. 19 f.

[14] *Ibid.*, p. 11.

[15] *Ibid.*, pp. 17 f.

[16] Cf. Wilhelm Süss, *Aristophanes und die Nachwelt*, Das Erbe der Alten, Heft II/III (Leipzig, 1911), p. 131; Süss makes this point here in reference to August Wilhelm Schlegel, but the defect is inherent in the Romantic approach to Aristophanes, originating with Friedrich.

[17] From the article "Athéisme" in the *Dictionnaire philosophique*, in *Oeuvres complètes de Voltaire*, ed. L. Moland (Paris, 1877-85), XVII, 469. Cf. Süss, *op. cit.*, pp. 88-120, for a survey of French and German dicta on Aristophanes in the eighteenth century.

[18] *Hamburgische Dramaturgie*, 91. Stück, *G. E. Lessings sämtliche Schriften*, ed. K. Lachmann and F. Muncker, 3rd ed. (Stuttgart, 1886-1924), X, 168 ff.

[19] *Ibid.*, VI, 14.

[20] Cf. Süss, *op. cit.*, pp. 106 ff.

[21] *Aristophanes: His Plays and His Influence* (Boston, 1925), p. 119.

[22] *Op. cit.*, pp. 126 f.

[23] "Magie, Karikatur, und Materialität sind die Mittel durch welche die moderne Komödie der alten Aristophanischen im Innern, wie durch demagogische Popularität im Äussern, ähnlich werden kann, und im Gozzi bis zur Erinnerung geworden ist. Das Wesen der komischen Kunst aber bleibt immer der enthusiastische Geist und die klassische Form." Minor, II, 243.

[24] Cf. also the 240th *Athenäum-Fragment*: "Im Aristophanes ist die Immoralität gleichsam legal, und in den Tragikern ist die Illegalität moralisch." *Ibid.*, p. 242.

[25] "Die Komödien des Aristophanes sind Kunstwerke, die sich von allen Seiten sehen lassen. Gozzi's Dramen haben einen Gesichtspunkt." *Ibid.*, p. 243.

[26] See Käthe Brodnitz, *Die vier Märchenkomödien von Ludwig Tieck* (diss. München, 1912), pp. 9 ff., 29 ff.; Hedwig Rusack, *Gozzi in Germany*, Columbia University Germanic Studies (New York, 1930), pp. 117-138.

[27] "Alle klassischen Dichtarten in ihrer strengen Reinheit sind jetzt lächerlich." Minor, II, 191.

[28] "Wer frisch vom Aristophanes, dem Olymp der Komödie, kommt, dem erscheint die romantische Persiflage wie eine lang ausgesponnene Faser aus einem Gewebe der Athene, wie eine Flocke himmlischen Feuers, von der das beste im Herabfallen auf die Erde verflog." *Ibid.*, p. 227.

[29] No. 13 of the *Lyceum* and No. 156 of the *Athenäum. Ibid.*, pp. 184, 227.

[30] E.g., the latter part of the 305th *Athenäum-Fragment, ibid.*, pp. 253 f.

[31] "Für die Shakespear-Briefe hab ich mir folgenden Plan entworfen
. . . 1) eine *Ouvertüre* von mir 2) eine *Charakteristik aller romantischen
Komödien* von Dir . . . 3) *Eine Theorie* der romantischen Komödie über-
haupt von mir, mit Vergleichung von Shakespear's Nebenmänner [*sic*],
Gozzi, die Spanier, Guarini etc. . . . 4) Von Dir. über den *tragischen
Gebrauch des Komischen* im Shakespear. Auch über den Antheil des
Komischen an seinen historischen Stücken. 5) Etwas Theoretisirendes als
Antistrophe darauf von mir. 6) Eine Charakteristik des Shakespearschen
Witzes überhaupt von Dir. 7) Eine des *romantischen Witzes* von mir, mit
Rücksicht auf Ariost, Cervantes &c. . . . Du müsstest däucht mich zwar
sehr speciell charakterisiren, wo dies gut schien, aber doch immer die Form
der romantischen Komödie, das Gemeinschaftliche aller Shakespearschen
Komödien und das Unterscheidende von den Tragödien im Auge behalten."
Friedrich Schlegels Briefe an seinen Bruder August Wilhelm, ed. Oskar
F. Walzel (Berlin, 1890), pp. 353 f. This work will hereafter be cited as
FSAW. Italics represent spaced type in source, except for "*aller romantischen Komödien*" in section 2) and "*romantischen*" in section 7), which
are in bold-faced type.

[32] "Möchtest Du doch auf meine Ueberzeugung genug achten, um im
Drama auch das *romantische* besonders zu constituiren. Ich überzeuge mich
immer mehr, dass dieses der einzige wahre Weg ist, und das sogar für die
Komödie. Das antike bleibt flach oder wird gelehrt und kann nur mytho-
logisch genommen bedeutend sein, wo es dann von selbst in das Gebiet der
esoterischen Poesie tritt. Das ganz moderne aber ist selbst für die Komödie
ein unwürdiger und steriler Stoff." *FSAW*, p. 496; italics represent spaced
type. It may be noted that, historically speaking, "das romantische" applies
generally to the Renaissance, "das ganz moderne," to the eighteenth century,
although national differences prevent a strictly chronological demarcation.

NOTES FOR CHAPTER THREE

[1] Ed. J. Minor, Deutsche Litteraturdenkmale, Vols. XVII-XIX (Heilbronn,
1884).

[2] *August Wilhelm von Schlegel's sämmtliche Werke*, ed. Eduard Böcking
(Leipzig, 1846-7), Vols. V and VI. This edition will hereafter be cited as
Böcking.

[3] *August Wilhelm Schlegels Vorlesungen über philosophische Kunstlehre
mit erläuternden Bemerkungen von Karl Christian Friedrich Krause*, ed.
A. Wünsche (Leipzig, 1911).

[4] Böcking, XII, 92-106.

[5] Böcking, V, 42 f., 178 ff.

[6] "Die neuere Komödie stellt zwar das Belustigende in Charakteren, con-
trastirenden Lagen und Zusammenstellungen derselben auf, und sie ist um
so komischer, je mehr das Zwecklose darin herrscht . . . ; aber unter allen
darin angebrachten Scherzen bleibt die Form der Darstellung selbst ernsthaft, das heisst an einen gewissen Zweck gesetzmässig gebunden. In der
alten Komödie hingegen ist diese scherzhaft, eine scheinbare Zwecklosig-
keit und Willkür herrscht darin, das Ganze des Kunstwerks ist ein einziger
grosser Scherz, der wieder eine ganze Welt von einzelnen Scherzen in sich
enthält, unter denen jeder seinen Platz für sich behaupten, und sich nicht
um die andern zu bekümmern scheint." *Ibid.*, pp. 181 f. Cf. also pp. 218 ff.

[7] "Man lasse sich dadurch nicht täuschen, dass die alten Komiker lebende
Menschen genannt und mit allen Umständen auf das Theater gebracht
haben, als ob sie deswegen in der That bestimmte Individuen dargestellt
hätten. Denn solche historische Personen haben bei ihnen immer eine alle-

gorische Bedeutung . . . Der komische Dichter versetzt wie der tragische
seine Personen in ein idealisches Element; aber nicht in eine Welt, wo die
Nothwendigkeit, sondern wo die Willkür des erfinderischen Witzes unbe-
dingt herrscht, und die Gesetze der Wirklichkeit aufgehoben sind. Er ist
folglich befugt, die Handlung so keck und phantastisch wie möglich zu
ersinnen; sie darf sogar unzusammenhängend und widersinnig sein . . ."
Ibid., pp. 183 f.

[8] "Da das Lustspiel die schöpferische Wirksamkeit der Phantasie beschränkt, so muss sie dem Verstande einen Ersatz dafür bieten, und dieser
liegt in der von ihm zu beurtheilenden Wahrscheinlichkeit des Dargestellten.
. . . Das Lustspiel muss ein treues Gemälde gegenwärtiger Sitten . . . sein
. . ." *Ibid.*, pp. 221 f.

[9] *Ibid.*, pp. 186 f.

[10] See quotation above, p. 31.

[11] Böcking, V, 184 f.

[12] See above, pp. 23 f.

[13] Böcking, V, 188 f.

[14] *Ibid.*, pp. 216 ff.

[15] Minor, I, 18.

[16] Böcking, V, 189 f.

[17] Böcking, XI, 23 f.

[18] Böcking, V, 183; *Schöne Literatur und Kunst*, II, 380.

[19] Böcking, V, 221 f., 230 ff.

[20] *Ibid.*, pp. 183 ff.

[21] *Ibid.*, pp. 184 f.

[22] *Ibid.*, p. 203.

[23] "Der Komiker muss überall durch die That die unbeschränkte Willkür
erklären, womit er befugt und gesonnen ist, sich über die bestehenden Ord-
nungen hinauszusetzen: durch die nahe Gegenwart gewinnen seine Erdich-
tungen einen ungleich dreisteren Charakter, und so entsteht jene unvergleich-
liche Tollheit der Freude und des Witzes, gegen welche die kühnsten Wag-
stücke des Erzählers nur nüchtern und beschränkt herauskommen." Böcking,
XII, 97.

[24] Böcking, V, 184.

[25] *Ibid.*, p. 193.

[26] "Da wir das Lustspiel als eine gemischte Gattung aus komischen und
tragischen, aus poetischen und prosaischen Elementen erklärt haben, so
erhellet schon von selbst, dass im Umfange dieser Gattung mehrere Unter-
arten stattfinden können, je nachdem einer oder der andere Bestandtheil
vorwaltet. Spielt der Dichter in scherzhafter Laune mit seinen eigenen
Erfindungen, so ensteht eine Posse; beschränkt er sich auf das Lächerliche
in den Lagen und Charakteren, mit möglichster Vermeidung aller ernst-
haften Beimischungen, ein reines Lustspiel; so wie der Ernst Feld gewinnt
. . . , so geht es in das belehrende oder rührende Schauspiel über . . ." *Ibid.*,
p. 225; my italics in translation.

[27] *Ibid.*, pp. 226 ff.

[28] *Ibid.*, pp. 228 ff.

[29] *Ibid.*, p. 228.

[30] Böcking, VI, 120 ff.

[31] "Wenn die Charaktere nur leicht angedeutet sind . . . ; wenn die
Verwickelung so auf die Spitze gestellt ist, dass sich die bunte Verwirrung
der Missverständnisse und Verlegenheiten in jedem Augenblicke lösen zu
müssen scheint, und doch der Knoten immer von neuem geschürzt wird: eine

solche Composition kann man wohl ein Intriguen-Stück nennen. Die französischen Kunstrichter haben es zur Mode gemacht, diese Art an Werth sehr tief unter das sogenannte Charakter-Stück herabzusetzen, vielleicht weil sie zu sehr darauf sehen, was man von einem Schauspiele behalten und mit sich nach Hause nehmen kann. Freilich löst sich am Ende das Intriguen-Stück gewissermassen in Nichts auf: aber warum sollte es nicht erlaubt sein, zuweilen ohne andern Zweck bloss sinnreich zu spielen?" Böcking, V, 227.

³² *Ibid.*, pp. 229 f. The quotation, on p. 230, reads: "Dann entsteht daraus das Komische der Willkür ... Hierin regt sich der Geist der alten Komödie; der bevorrechtete Lustigmacher, den fast alle Bühnen unter verschiedenen Namen gehabt ..., hat etwas von der ausgelassenen Begeisterung, und somit auch von den Rechten des unbeschränkt freien alten Komikers geerbt; zum sichern Beweise, dass die alte Komödie ... nicht etwa eine griechische Eigenheit war, sondern dass ihr Wesen in der Natur der Sache gegründet ist."

³³ ". . . eine bunte Wunderposse, sprühend von dem so selten in Frankreich einheimischen phantastischen Witz, beseelt von jenem heitern Scherz, der, wiewohl bis zum Taumel der Fröhlichkeit ausgelassen, harmlos um Alles und über Alles hingaukelt. Wir möchten es eine zierliche und sinnvolle Tollheit nennen; ein anschauliches Beispiel, wie die Gattung des Aristophanes ... mit Vermeidung ihrer Anstössigkeiten und ohne persönlichen Spott, auf unsrer Bühne erscheinen dürfte." Böcking, VI, 128 f. *Le Roy de Cocagne* was published in Paris in 1719. See the synopsis and excerpts in E. Lintilhac, *La Comédie, dix-huitième siècle*, Histoire générale du théâtre en France, IV (Paris [1909]), pp. 140-155.

³⁴ Böcking, X, 93 f.

³⁵ Böcking, VI, 415.

³⁶ *Ibid.*, pp. 107 ff.

³⁷ Böcking, XII, 99.

³⁸ *Schöne Literatur und Kunst*, III, 59.

³⁹ Böcking, V, 363 ff.; VI, 403 f.

⁴⁰ Böcking, VI, 201 ff.

⁴¹ *Ibid.*, pp. 284 f.

⁴² "Falstaff ist der angenehmste und unterhaltendste Taugenichts, der je geschildert worden. . . . Man sieht, dass seine zärtliche Besorgniss für ihn selbst ohne alle Beimischung von Tücke gegen Andre ist; nur in der behaglichen Ruhe seiner Sinnlichkeit will er nicht gestört werden ... Er ist so überzeugt, dass die Rolle, die er spielt, nur unter dem Deckmantel des Witzes durchschlüpfen kann, dass er auch sich selbst gegenüber niemals ganz ernsthaft ist, und seinen Lebenswandel, seine Verhältnisse zu Andern und seine sinnliche Philosophie auf eine lustige Weise einkleidet." Böcking, VI, 282.

⁴³ *Ibid.*, pp. 214 f.

⁴⁴ *Ibid.*, pp. 215 ff.

⁴⁵ *Ibid.*, pp. 217 ff. The quotation, on p. 217, reads: "Es ist eine muthwillige Gaukelei, ein ganzes Füllhorn der muntersten Scherze ist darin ausgeschüttet. . . . Die Funken des Witzes sprühen, so, dass sie ein wahres Feuerwerk bilden . . ."

⁴⁶ *Ibid.*, pp. 394 f.

⁴⁷ "Auch diejenigen Schauspiele Calderons in modernen Sitten, die am meisten zum Ton des gemeinen Lebens herabsteigen, fesseln durch irgend einen phantastischen Zauber, und können nicht ganz für Lustspiele im gewöhnlichen Sinne des Wortes gelten. Wir haben gesehen, dass die sogenannten Lustspiele Shakspeares immer aus zwei fremdartigen Theilen

zusammengesetzt sind, dem komischen, welcher in englischen Sitten gehalten ist . . . , und dem romantischen, auf irgend einen südlichen Schauplatz hinaus verlegten, weil der einheimische Boden nicht dichterisch genug dazu war. In Spanien hingegen konnte das damalige nationale Costüm noch von der idealen Seite gefasst werden." Böcking, VI, 393.

[48] Böcking, VI, 160 ff. The quotation, on p. 161, reads: "Die antike Kunst und Poesie geht auf strenge Sonderung des Ungleichartigen, die romantische gefällt sich in unauflöslichen Mischungen; alle Entgegengesetzten, Natur und Kunst, Poesie und Prosa, Ernst und Scherz, Erinnerung und Ahndung, Geistigkeit und Sinnlichkeit, das Irdische und Göttliche, Leben und Tod, verschmilzt sie auf das innigste mit einander."

[49] See above, p. 33.

[50] Friedrich Schlegel could not have accepted this proposition. See Marie Joachimi-Dege, *Probleme*, p. 169.

[51] "Wo das eigentlich Tragische eintritt, hört freilich alle Ironie auf: allein von dem eingestandnen Scherz der Komödie an bis dahin, wo die Unterwerfung sterblicher Wesen unter ein unvermeidliches Schicksal den strengen Ernst fordert, giebt es eine Menge menschlicher Verhältnisse, die allerdings . . . mit Ironie betrachtet werden dürfen." Böcking, VI, 198 f.

[52] *Ibid.*, p. 199.

[53] *Ibid.*, p. 396.

[54] Böcking, V, 365 f.

[55] "Ein unendlich reizender Widerspruch ist in diesem Geist der Liebe, aber zugleich die Anlage zur Ironie, welche aus dem Bewusstseyn des Unerreichbaren, statt zu niederschlagendem Ernst überzugehn, einen leisen Scherz macht." *Schöne Literatur und Kunst*, III, 109.

[56] See Marie Joachimi-Dege, *Probleme*, pp. 167 ff.

[57] See "Schlegel's Poetic Irony," *GR*, XXVI, 182 f.

[58] "Niemand hat so wie er den leisen Selbstbetrug geschildert, die halb selbstbewusste Heuchelei gegen sich, womit auch edle Gemüther die in der menschlichen Natur fast unvermeidliche Eindrängung selbstischer Triebfedern verkleiden. Diese geheime Ironie der Charakteristik ist bewundernswürdig als ein Abgrund von Scharfsinn, aber dem Enthusiasmus thut sie wehe. Dahin kommt man also, wenn man das Unglück gehabt hat, die Menschheit zu durchschauen, und ausser der traurigen Wahrheit, dass keine Tugend und Grösse ganz rein und ächt sei, und dem gefährlichen Irrthum, als stände das Höchste zu erreichen, bleibt uns keine Wahl übrig. Hier spüre ich, während er die innigsten Rührungen erregt, in dem Dichter selbst eine gewisse Kälte, aber die eines überlegenen Geistes, der den Kreiss des menschlichen Daseins durchlaufen, und das Gefühl überlebt hat." Böcking, VI, 197 f.

[59] See his allusion to the marriage at the end of *Henry V*, *ibid.*, p. 291.

[60] "Die Ironie bezieht sich aber bei'm Shakspeare nicht bloss auf die einzelnen Charaktere, sondern häufig auf das Ganze der Handlung. Die meisten Dichter . . . nehmen Partei, und verlangen von den Lesern blinden Glauben für ihre Bemühungen zu erheben oder herabzusetzen. . . . Wenn hingegen der Dichter zuweilen durch eine geschickte Wendung die weniger glänzende Kehrseite der Münze nach vorne dreht, so setzt er sich mit dem auserlesenen Kreiss der Einsichtsvollen unter seinen Lesern oder Zuschauern in ein verstohlnes Einverständniss; er zeigt ihnen, dass er ihre Einwendungen vorhergesehen und im voraus zugegeben habe; dass er nicht selbst in dem dargestellten Gegenstande befangen sei, sondern frei über ihm schwebe, und dass er den schönen unwiderstehlich anziehenden Schein, den er selbst hervorgezaubert, wenn er anders wollte, unerbittlich vernichten könnte." Böcking, VI, 198.

[61] "Ein in die Darstellung selbst hineingelegtes mehr oder weniger leise angedeutetes Eingeständniss ihrer übertreibenden Einseitigkeit in dem Antheil der Phantasie und Empfindung . . . , wodurch also das Gleichgewicht wieder hergestellt wird." Böcking, V, 366; my italics in translation.

[62] "Es ist eine Parodie der Ritterromane . . . Aber die eigentlich sinnreiche Neuheit des Stückes besteht in der Zusammenstellung dieser Ironie über einen chimärischen Missbrauch der Poesie mit einer andern gerade entgegengesetzten Ironie über die Unfähigkeit, irgend eine Dichtung und die dramatische Form insbesondere zu begreifen. . . . Der Gewürzkrämer und seine Frau . . . repräsentieren eine ganze Gattung, nämlich die unpoetischen und von Kunstsinn entblössten Zuschauer. Die Illusion wird bei ihnen zum leidentlichen Irrthum, das Vorgestellte wirkt auf sie als wäre es wirklich . . . Auf der andern Seite zeigen sie sich aller ächten Illusion, d. h. der lebhaften Versetzung in den Geist der Dichtung unfähig . . ." Böcking, VI, 351 f.; my italics in translation.

[63] Böcking, V, 194.

NOTES FOR CHAPTER FOUR

[1] *Ludwig Tieck's nachgelassene Schriften*, ed. Rudolf Köpke (Leipzig, 1855), I, 21-75. Köpke gives 1790 as the date. Tieck's authorship, which had been disputed, was established beyond doubt by Professor E. H. Zeydel in his article, "Das Reh — ein Jugendwerk Ludwig Tiecks," *Euphorion*, XXIX, (1928), 93-108.

[2] *Schriften*, XII, 1-154.

[3] *Ibid.*, pp. 355-420.

[4] *Schriften*, V, 7-152.

[5] Böcking, XI, 136 ff.; the part of the review pertaining to *Der gestiefelte Kater* will be discussed in ch. vi.

[6] E.g., "Ich hätte mich lieber nach Regeln rühren lassen," *Schriften*, V, 29.

[7] *Ibid.*, p. 94.

[8] Köpke, who published the play in *Tieck's nachgelassene Schriften* (I, 76-126) and provided the title, suggests 1795 as the likely date of origin (*ibid.*, pp. xii f.).

[9] As demonstrated by Paul Schlenther, *Frau Gottsched und die bürgerliche Komödie* (Berlin, 1886), Gottsched was not entirely successful in this endeavor even in Germany. At his real home in Vienna, Hanswurst and numerous progeny flourished for another century.

[10] See *Nachgelassene Schriften*, I, 79, 97, 125.

[11] *Ibid.*, p. 125.

[12] *Ibid.*, pp. 91, 125.

[13] *Ibid.*, pp. 78 f.

[14] *Ibid.*, pp. 101 f., 117.

[15] *Ibid.*, p. 88.

[16] *Schriften*, XIII, 239-266.

[17] *Ibid.*, p. 261.

[18] Tieck's letter of July 5, 1797, to Friedrich Nicolai reveals that two editions had already been published by that date. See *Letters of Ludwig Tieck, Hitherto Unpublished*, ed. E. H. Zeydel, Percy Matenko, and R. H. Fife (New York and London, 1937), pp. 22 f. This original version, of which there were several editions, is reprinted in *Satiren und Parodien*, ed. Andreas Müller, Deutsche Literatur: Reihe Romantik, IX (Leipzig, 1935), 13-62, to be cited hereafter as *GK*. It is much shorter and more effective than the version revised for the collection *Phantasus*, which is printed in Tieck's *Schriften*, V, 161-280.

[19] The Spectator "Bötticher" caricatures the trivial histrionic analysis of K. A. Böttiger, *Entwicklung des Ifflandschen Spieles* (Leipzig, 1796). See quotation below, p. 52; *Schriften*, I, xvi f.; introduction of A. Müller, *GK*, p. 7. This is the sole instance of direct personal satire in *Der gestiefelte Kater*.

[20] Quoted below, p. 53.

[21] *GK*, pp. 33 f., 49.

[22] "Pfui! schäme dich, Hinz!—Ist es nicht die Pflicht des Edeln, sich und seine Neigungen dem Glück seiner Mitgeschöpfe aufzuopfern? Dies ist die Ursach', warum wir leben, und wer das nicht kann — oh, ihm wäre besser, dass er nie geboren wäre." *GK*, p. 35. The translation is that of Lillie Winter in *The German Classics*, ed. Kuno Francke (Albany, n. d.), IV, 220, with some emendations of my own. This translation will hereafter be cited as *PB*.

[23] *GK*, pp. 39 f.

[24] *Popanz.* See *GK*, p. 28.

[25] *GK*, p. 58.

[26] The attempt of J. Wolf to trace satiric allusions to individuals in European politics and the Prussian court ("Les Allusions politiques dans le 'Chat botté' de Ludwig Tieck," *Revue germanique*, V [1909], 158-201) is to be cited only as a classic example of critical nonsense.

[27] The present investigation nowhere attempts a searching analysis of the sources of the comic or ludicrous in Tieck's creation but merely points out those qualities which distinguish it as *fantastic* comedy. L. Faerber, *Das Komische bei Ludwig Tieck* (diss. Giessen, 1917), catalogues the comic episodes in all of Tieck's writings according to the esthetic principles of T. H. Lipps.

[28] Allusion to Kotzebue's *Negersklaven* (1796); see Müller's note, *GK*, p. 237.

[29] "*Wiesener.* Die Husaren gefielen mir besonders, es riskieren die Leute selten, Pferde aufs Theater zu bringen—und warum nicht? Sie haben oft mehr Verstand als die Menschen. Ich mag lieber ein gutes Pferd sehn als so manchen Menschen in den neueren Stücken.

"*Nachbar.* Im Kotzebue die Mohren—ein Pferd ist am Ende nichts als eine andere Art von Mohren. . . . ich möchte wohl ein ganzes Stück von lauter Husaren sehn—ich mag die Kavallerie so gern." *GK*, p. 30; *PB*, p. 214.

[30] "Ich habe nur immer noch das vortreffliche Spiel des Mannes im Kopfe, der den Kater darstellt. — Welches Studium! Welche Feinheit! Welche Beobachtung! Welcher Anzug! . . . haben Sie wohl bemerkt, dass es nicht einer von den schwarzen Katern ist? Nein, im Gegenteil, er ist fast ganz weiss und hat nur einige schwarze Flecke, das drückt seine Gutmütigkeit ganz vortrefflich aus, man sieht gleichsam den Gang des ganzen Stücks, alle Empfindungen, die es erregen soll, schon in diesem Pelze." *GK*, pp. 30 f.; *PB*, pp. 214 f.

[31] *GK*, p. 43, *PB*, p. 230.

[32] *GK*, p. 45.

[33] *GK*, pp. 33 f.

[34] "*Prinzessin.* Mein allergnädigster Herr Vater, ich habe immer geglaubt, dass mein Herz erst einige Empfindungen zeigen müsse, ehe ich meinen Nacken in das Joch des Ehestandes beugte. Denn eine Ehe ohne Liebe, sagt man, ist die wahre Hölle auf Erden.

"*König.* Recht so, meine liebe Tochter. Ach, wohl, wohl . . . eine Hölle auf Erden! Ach, wenn ich doch nicht darüber mitsprechen könnte! . . . Deine Mutter, meine höchstselige Gemahlin — ach, Prinzessin, sieh, die Tränen stehn mir noch auf meinen alten Tagen in den Augen—, sie war

eine gute Fürstin, sie trug die Krone mit einer unbeschreiblichen Majestät
—aber mir hat sie gar wenig Ruhe gelassen . . . Was hab' ich gelitten!
Kein Tag verging ohne Zank, ich konnte nicht in Ruhe schlafen . . . Und
doch sehnt sich mein Geist, verewigte Klotilde, jetzt zuweilen nach dir
zurück—es beisst mir in den Augen—ich bin ein rechter alter Narr." *GK*,
pp. 23 f.; *PB*, pp. 206 f.

[35] *"Prinzessin.* . . . Sagt mir doch einmal, guter Bauer, warum haut Ihr
denn da das Stroh so um?

"Kunz (lachend). Das ist ja die Ernte, Mamsell Königin, das Getreide.

"König. Das Getreide?—Wozu braucht Ihr denn das?

"Kunz (lachend). Daraus wird ja das Brot gebacken.

"König. Bitt' ich dich ums Himmels willen, Tochter—daraus wird Brot
gebacken!—Wer sollte wohl auf solche Streiche kommen?—Die Natur ist
doch etwas Wunderbares." *GK*, p. 55; *PB*, p. 245.

[36] *GK*, pp. 56 f.

[37] *GK*, pp. 53 f.

[38] *GK*, p. 33.

[39] *GK*, p. 32.

[40] *GK*, p. 39.

[41] *GK*, p. 42.

[42] "Seinem langen weissen Barte nach sollte es ein Greis sein, und sein
ganz mit Haaren bedecktes Gesicht sollte einen darin fast bestärken, aber
dann hat er wieder so muntre jugendliche Augen, einen so dienstfertigen
geschmeidigen Rücken, dass man an ihm irre wird." *GK*, pp. 36 f.; *PB*,
pp. 222 f.

[43] See above, p. 51.

[44] *GK*, p. 21.

[45] *"Amtmann.* Mit Ihrer gütigen Erlaubnis, ich zittre und bebe vor Dero
furchtbarem Anblick.

"Popanz. Oh, das ist noch lange nicht meine entsetzlichste Gestalt.

"Amtmann. Ich kam eigentlich—in Sachen—um Sie zu bitten, sich meiner
gegen meinen Nachbarn anzunehmen—ich hatte auch diesen Beutel mit-
gebracht—aber der Anblick des Herrn Gesetzes ist mir zu schrecklich.

"(Popanz verwandelt sich plötzlich in eine Maus und sitzt in einer Ecke.)

"Amtmann. Wo ist denn der Popanz geblieben?

"Popanz (mit einer feinen Stimme). Legen Sie nur das Geld auf den
Tisch dort hin, ich sitze hier, um Sie nicht zu erschrecken." *GK*, p. 57; *PB*,
pp. 247 f.

[46] "Gelt, Freund, das sind Kunststücke?" *GK*, p. 58; *PB*, p. 249.

[47] *GK*, pp. 21, 54.

[48] *GK*, p. 55.

[49] *GK*, p. 33, and editor's note, p. 237.

[50] *GK*, p. 37, and editor's note, p. 237.

[51] *GK*, p. 25, and editor's note, p. 237.

[52] *GK*, p. 29, and editor's note, p. 237.

[53] *"Hinze.* Was seid Ihr für ein Landsmann?

"Hanswurst. Leider nur ein Deutscher. Meine Landsleute wurden um
eine gewisse Zeit so klug, dass sie allen Spass ordentlich bei Strafe ver-
boten, wo man mich nur gewahr ward, gab man mir unausstehliche Ekel-
namen, als: abgeschmackt, unanständig, bizarr — wer über mich lachte,
wurde ebenso wie ich verfolgt, und so musst' ich in die Verbannung
wandern." *GK*, p. 38; *PB*, p. 225, where Hanswurst is named "Jackpud-
ding."

[54] See above, p. 54.

[55] "Das macht, es ist eine Natur, die noch nicht idealisiert ist, die Phantasie muss sie erst veredeln." *GK*, p. 54; *PB*, p. 243.

[56] Their relation to the outermost sphere would depend on the judgment of the actual producer, but Tieck himself thought of a small theater in which the whole orchestra would be given over to these Spectators. *Schriften*, I, xx.

[57] "*König*. . . . Aber noch eins, sagen Sie nur, da Sie so weit weg wohnen, wie Sie unsre Sprache so geläufig sprechen können?
"*Nathanael* [*von Malsinki*]. Still!
"*König*. Wie?
"*Nathanael*. Still! Still!
"*König*. Ich versteh' nicht.
"*Nathanael* (leise zu ihm). Sein Sie doch ja damit ruhig, denn sonst merkt es ja am Ende das Publikum da unten, dass das eben sehr unnatürlich ist.
"*König*. Schadet nichts, es hat vorher geklatscht, und da kann ich ihm schon etwas bieten.
"*Nathanael*. Sehn Sie, es geschieht ja bloss dem Drama zu Gefallen, dass ich Ihre Sprache rede, denn sonst ist es allerdings unbegreiflich." *GK*, p. 27; *PB*, pp. 210 f.

[58] *GK*, pp. 42 f., 59 f. These spectacles parody Scenes 12, 28, and 30 in Act II of Schikaneder's libretto to Mozart's *Zauberflöte*. Here Tieck's satire is directed against a Viennese theatrical tradition which was a product of the Baroque rather than of the Enlightenment. Tieck's failure to appreciate and to exploit in a positive sense the popular appeal of a colorful, spectacular staging for fantastic farce was one reason why his own could not become a living theatrical tradition like that of the Viennese suburbs.

[59] *GK*, pp. 44 ff.

[60] This is a stage functionary whose job it is to pacify the audience by means of spectacles, ballets, and music; *PB* has "peacemaker."

[61] "Wenn es nur nicht von hier so weit nach dem Palast des Königs wäre, so holt' ich den Besänftiger, . . . aber bin ich nicht ein Tor?—Ich bin ganz in Verwirrung geraten—das ist ja hier das Theater, und der Besänftiger muss irgendwo zwischen den Kulissen stecken . . . " *GK*, p. 59; *PB*, p. 249.

[62] "*Leander*. Das Thema meiner Behauptung ist, dass ein neuerlich erschienenes Stück, mit dem Namen: *Der gestiefelte Kater*, ein gutes Stück sei.
"*Hanswurst*. Das ist eben das, was ich leugne.

"*Leander*. Das Stück ist, wenn nicht ganz vortrefflich, doch in einigen Rücksichten zu loben.
"*Hanswurst*. In keiner Rücksicht.
"*Leander*. Ich behaupte, es ist Witz darin.
"*Hanswurst*. Ich behaupte, es ist keiner darin.

"*Leander*. Manche Charaktere sind gut durchgeführt.
"*Hanswurst*. Kein einziger.
"*Leander*. So ist, wenn ich auch alles übrige fallen lasse, das Publikum gut darin gezeichnet.
"*Hanswurst*. Ein Publikum hat nie einen Charakter.
"*Leander*. Über diese Frechheit möcht' ich fast erstaunen.
"*Hanswurst* (gegen das Parterre). Ist es nicht ein närrischer Mensch? Wir stehn nun beide auf du und du und sympathisieren in Ansehung des Geschmacks, und er will gegen meine Meinung behaupten, das Publikum im 'Gestiefelten Kater' sei wenigstens gut gezeichnet.
"*Fischer*. Das Publikum? Es kömmt [*sic*] ja kein Publikum in dem Stücke vor.

"*Leander*. Ich werde konfus—aber ich lasse dir noch nicht den Sieg." *GK*, pp. 50 ff.; *PB*, pp. 239 f.

[63] See Hedwig Rusack, *Gozzi in Germany*, pp. 123 ff.

[64] "Mein Nachbar ist so nicht mein guter Freund, und er hat ein vortreffliches Land, alle Rosinen kommen von dort her, das möcht' ich gar zu gerne haben . . ." *GK*, p. 27; *PB*, p. 210.

[65] *GK*, pp. 35 ff., 41.

[66] As one evidence of this, Professor Zeydel cites the allusion to "unser würdiger gestiefelter Kater" in a letter to Goethe by Schiller, who rarely expressed admiration for any product of German Romanticism. See Edwin H. Zeydel, *Ludwig Tieck, the German Romanticist* (Princeton, 1935), pp. 88 f.

[67] Tieck had already emulated this trait of Shakespeare's fools in the court jester of his *Blaubart*.

[68] When the Spectators clamor for a curtain call by the closing stage-set, Hanswurst courteously thanks them in the latter's name. *GK*, p. 61.

[69] See above, pp. 36 f.

[70] "Als ich Dero Pochen vernahm—noch nie hat mich etwas dermassen erschreckt, ich bin noch bleich und zittre und begreife selbst nicht, wie ich zu der Kühnheit komme, so vor Ihnen zu erscheinen." *GK*, p. 17; *PB*, p. 198.

[71] *GK*, p. 62.

[72] "Ich wollte einen Versuch machen, durch Laune, wenn sie mir gelungen ist, durch Heiterkeit, durch wirkliche Possen zu belustigen, da uns unsre neuesten Stücke so selten zum Lachen Gelegenheit geben." *GK*, p. 17; *PB*, p. 198.

[73] "Ich hatte den Versuch gemacht, Sie alle in die entfernten Empfindungen Ihrer Kinderjahre zurückzuversetzen, dass Sie so das dargestellte Märchen empfunden hätten, ohne es doch für etwas Wichtigeres zu halten, als es sein sollte." *GK*, p. 62 (the Epilogue is not included in *PB*).

[74] See *GK*, p. 25.

[75] See above, p. 34.

[76] See Zeydel, *Ludwig Tieck, the German Romanticist*, p. 89; Ignaz Gentges, "Tiecks Märchenbühne (Die Geste als Wort und Gebärde im Drama Ludwig Tiecks)," *Das deutsche Theater, Jahrbuch für Drama und Bühne*, I (1922-23), 144; also the list of German stage productions for the season 1921-22 in the same volume, p. 415.

[77] *Schriften*, I, xx.

[78] See Gentges, *op. cit.*, pp. 148-153.

[79] Tieck's correspondence with Friedrich Nicolai reveals that the manuscript of *Die verkehrte Welt* was in the latter's hands on December 19, 1797, and it was probably written during the few weeks immediately preceding that date. See *Briefe an Ludwig Tieck*, ed. Karl von Holtei (Breslau, 1864), III, 58 ff.; *Letters of Ludwig Tieck*, pp. 23 f.; Zeydel, *op. cit.*, pp. 89 f. Tieck told Solger in 1816 that he had written the play in a few days. *Tieck and Solger, the Complete Correspondence*, ed. Percy Matenko (New York and Berlin, 1933), p. 211.

[80] He mentioned the idea of a play on Weise's theme to Nicolai in 1796. *Letters of Ludwig Tieck*, pp. 19 f.

[81] *Schriften*, V, 304.

[82] *Ibid.*, pp. 303, 325 ff.

[83] *Ibid.*, pp. 329 f.

[84] That this style is, in part, deliberate satire of rationalistic intellectualism does not justify its indiscriminate use in comedy.

[85] However, the contrast would be less striking if, instead of the original short version of *Der gestiefelte Kater*, we were to base our comparison upon the unhappily revised and expanded text published in *Phantasus*. Professor H. W. Hewett-Thayer's comparison of the three published versions of *Die*

verkehrte Welt discloses that in this case the defects, though perhaps amplified in successive revisions, were already manifest at the start. "Tieck's Revision of His Satirical Comedies," *Germanic Review*, XII (1937), 154-160, 162 ff.

[86] *Schriften*, V, 313 ff.

[87] *Ibid.*, pp. 389-398.

[88] *Ibid.*, pp. 352-373.

[89] *"Fremder.* Guten Morgen, Herr Wirth.

"Wirth. Diener, Diener von Ihnen gnädiger Herr.—Wer in aller Welt sind Sie, dass Sie inkognito reisen und bei mir einkehren? Sie sind gewiss noch aus der alten Schule; gelt, so ein Mann vom alten Schlage, vielleicht aus dem Englischen übersetzt?

"Fremder. Ich bin weder gnädiger Herr, noch reise ich incognito.—Kann ich diesen Tag und die Nacht hier logiren?

"Wirth. Mein ganzes Haus steht Ihnen zu Befehl.—Aber, im Ernst, wollen Sie hier in der Gegend keine Familie unvermutheterweise glücklich machen? oder plötzlich heirathen? oder eine Schwester aufsuchen.

"Fremder. Nein, mein Freund.

"Wirth. Da werden Sie wenig Beifall finden." (*Ibid.*, pp. 321 f.)

[90] The fondness of Aristophanes for "a world turned topsy-turvy" is mentioned by Louis E. Lord, *Aristophanes, His Plays and His Influence* (Boston, 1925), p. 18.

[91] Henri Bergson, *Le Rire*, 8th ed. (Paris, 1912), pp. 95 ff.

[92] He may call forth "eine umgekehrte Natur, ein lustiges Chaos." Böcking, XII, 95.

[93] Christian Weise, *Lustspiel von der verkehrten Welt, Neue Jugend-, Lust-: Das ist Drey Schauspiele*, III (Frankfurt and Leipzig, 1684). Cf. F. Riederer, *Ludwig Tiecks Beziehungen zur deutschen Literatur des 17. Jahrhunderts* (diss. Greifswald, 1915), pp. 81-92.

[94] *Lustspiel von der verkehrten Welt*, pp. 56 ff.

[95] *Schriften*, V, 375 ff.

[96] *Ibid.*, p. 435.

[97] *Ibid.*, p. 303.

[98] *Ibid.*, pp. 300, 324.

[99] *Ibid.*, pp. 334 f., 340 f.

[100] *Ibid.*, pp. 385 ff.

[101] *Ibid.*, pp. 380 ff.

[102] *Ibid.*, pp. 326 ff.

[103] Tieck himself relates that the response to his reading of the comedy in the salon of Frau Unger, wife of the publisher, was "ein steinharter, unbezwinglicher Ernst," instead of the laughter he had expected. *Schriften*, I, xxiii.

[104] *Ibid.*, p. xxv.

[105] *Eduard Mörikes sämtliche Werke*, ed. R. Krauss (Leipzig [1909]), V, 118 ff.

[106] See Hewett-Thayer, *GR*, XII, 154 ff.

[107] Minor, II, 220; quoted in part below, p. 107 and note 21, ch. vi.

[108] Tieck's own utterances on the chronology of *Zerbino*'s genesis are conflicting. See *Schriften*, X, 1; *Tieck and Solger*, p. 211; Hewett-Thayer, *GR*, XII, 147 f.

[109] "Gewissermassen eine Fortsetzung des gestiefelten Katers" is the subtitle. *Schriften*, X, 1.

[110] *Schriften*, X, 176-187.

[111] *Schriften,* VI, xl ff.

[112] *Schriften,* X, 131 ff., 154 ff.

[113] *Ibid.,* pp. 249 f.

[114] *Ibid.,* pp. 328-338.

[115] *Ibid.,* p. 140.

[116] *Ibid.,* pp. 197 ff.

[117] *Ibid.,* pp. 206 ff.

[118] *Ibid.,* pp. 257-293.

[119] "Die *Verkehrte Welt* ist richtiger, ich möchte sagen, philosophischer gebaut, dem *Zerb*[*ino*] thäte jene Nothwendigkeit gut, die dort die verschiedenen Kreise in Bewegung setzt, und Willkühr, Tollheit, Zufall besser vereinigt . . ." Letter of April 1, 1816, *Tieck and Solger,* p. 211.

[120] *Schriften,* XI, 145-268.

[121] H. Rusack, *Gozzi in Germany,* pp. 130 ff., notes a considerable resemblance to *Il Mostro turchino.*

[122] *Schriften,* XI, liii ff.

[123] *Die romantische Schule,* p. 90.

[124] A modest success was achieved in the same endeavor by a younger German romantic poet, Eduard Mörike, in his fantastic operetta, *Die Regenbrüder,* composed by Ignaz Lachner and produced in Stuttgart in 1839. (See Harry Maync, *Eduard Mörike,* 5th ed. [Stuttgart, 1944], pp. 300 f.). With Mörike, supernatural personifications of natural forces display the homely comic foibles of peasant youth and put their fantastic endowments to very human uses. He thus unites, rather than opposes, earthly reality and poetic imagination.

[125] *Schriften,* XI, 149 f. This generalization, Tieck explains here, is based on the principle that "alles possierlich erscheint, was wir unabgesondert in seiner Gattung darstellen wollen." In almost identical terms, Henri Bergson declares: "Toute ressemblance à un type a quelque chose de comique" (*Le Rire,* p. 152). Tieck had already discussed the importance of generalized characters against a fantastic background in the earlier essay, "Shakespeares Behandlung des Wunderbaren," *Kritische Schriften* (Leipzig, 1848-52), I, 55-62.

[126] *Schriften,* XI, 156, 192.

[127] *Ibid.,* p. 149.

[128] *Ibid.,* p. 235.

[129] *Ibid.,* pp. 226 f.

[130] *Ibid.,* p. 160.

[131] *Ibid.,* pp. 172, 191 f., 195.

[132] *Ibid.,* pp. 210 ff.

[133] *Ibid.,* p. 259.

[134] *Nachgelassene Schriften,* I, 127-159.

[135] *Ibid.,* p. 139; the same pun recurs on the next page.

[136] *Ibid.,* p. 138.

[137] *Ibid.,* pp. 141 f. He appears as "Der Bötticher."

[138] *Ibid.,* p. 142.

[139] Closely similar themes and techniques are to be found in *The Devil Is an Ass* and in *Götter, Helden, und Wieland.* See H. Stanger, "Der Einfluss Ben Jonsons auf Ludwig Tieck," *Studien zur vergleichenden Litteraturgeschichte,* II (1902), 37-79.

[140] E.g., the last line in *Nachgelassene Schriften,* I, 131.

[141] *Ibid.,* pp. 150 ff.

[142] *Ibid.,* p. 154.

143 *Ibid.*, p. 155.

144 *Ibid.*, p. 153.

145 *Schriften*, II, 327-362.

146 *Schriften*, V, 487-595.

147 See Eduard Mörike, *Briefe*, ed. Friedrich Seebass (Tübingen [1939]), pp. 59, 65 f.

148 See his letter to Tieck of February 20, 1833. *Ibid.*, pp. 389 f.

149 See the mock-heroic ballads of the court poet Persiwein. *Schriften*, V, 589-594.

150 *Ibid.*, pp. 569-573, 582, 587 f., 594 f.

151 Ludvig Holberg's *Ulysses of Ithaca*, which had ridiculed the implausibilities of baroque melodrama from this same standpoint, originally inspired Tieck to violate theatrical illusion with the opposite objective, the mockery of sober common sense, in *Der gestiefelte Kater*. See *Schriften*, I, viii. Tieck had always been fond of Holberg, but by the time he wrote *Däumchen* he had even swung around to a similar position in matters of taste.

152 *Schriften*, V, 576 f.

153 However, Aristophanes usually parodies particular works and passages. See Charlton C. Jernigan, *Incongruity in Aristophanes* (diss. Duke University, 1939), pp. 25-40.

154 *Schriften*, V, 501 ff.

155 *Ibid.*, pp. 509 f.

156 "Ich denke überhaupt manchmal darüber nach,—gebt mir jetzt die andre Keule, der Hammel ist auch verwünscht klein,—ich denke wohl so drüber nach, sag ich (denn ich denke gern), dass es denn doch wohl anders schmecken muss und besser, . . . einen guten Freund, oder eine Geliebte aufzufressen; besonders in der Zeit der ersten Liebe, wo man noch weniger dreist ist, sich anzunähern scheut, wo unser ganzes Wesen in Sehnsucht zittert.—Gebt mir mal den andern Humpen Wein.—Semmelziege, was meint Ihr?" *Ibid.*, p. 549.

157 *Schriften*, I, xliii.

158 See *Immermanns Werke*, ed. W. Dietjen (Berlin, etc. [1912]), II, 209.

159 *Tieck and Solger*, pp. 105 f.

160 He sets this up as the cardinal principle of personal satire in his essay, "Bemerkungen über Parteilichkeit, Dummheit und Bosheit, bei Gelegenheit der Herren Falk, Merkel und des Lustspiels 'Camäleon'" (*Nachgelassene Schriften*, II, 35-93), to which reference will be made in the next chapter.

161 It is true that a certain structural pattern handed down in the tradition of Attic comedy is recognizable in most comedies of Aristophanes, but this pattern cannot be called a *dramatic* structure, because it does not contribute to the evolution of a conflict or the building up of suspense. It is essential neither to the comic nor to the satiric purposes of Aristophanes, and he therefore frequently modifies, and on occasion virtually disregards it. See Lord, *op. cit.*, pp. 14-18.

162 *Aristophanes, with the English Translation of Benjamin B. Rogers*, The Loeb Classical Library (London and New York, 1924), II, 297. All quotations of Aristophanes are from this translation, to which reference will hereafter be made by line numbers.

163 See translator's footnote *b, ibid.*, I, 293.

164 See translator's footnote *b, ibid.*, I, 42.

165 See above, p. 64.

166 See above, p. 77.

NOTES FOR CHAPTER FIVE

[1] *Das Buch über Shakespeare*, ed. Henry Lüdeke, Neudrucke deutscher Literaturwerke des 18. and 19. Jahrhunderts, I (Halle, 1920), pp. 1-364. This work will hereafter be cited as *Shakespeare*.

[2] *Shakespeare*, pp. 365-394.

[3] This chapter will focus its attention upon the second, Romantic, period and on those later critical utterances which continue in the Romantic vein. A general exposition of the criticism relating to comedy in the first and third periods may be found in my dissertation in the library of the University of California at Berkeley, "Ludwig Tieck's Contribution in Theory and Practice to the German Romanticists' Conception of Comedy," (1941), pp. 57-84, 243-300.

[4] *Schriften*, XIII, 267-334.

[5] See above, ch. iv, note 160.

[6] *Kritische Schriften*, I, 217-232.

[7] *Shakespeare*, pp. 365, 395 ff.

[8] "Dasjenige, was meine Jugend bedrängte, die Widerwärtigkeiten in der Zeit, die mich gestört hatten . . . , trat jetzt . . . in dem magischen Zaubergemälde der Poesie auf. Der heitre Scherz musste sich dieser Gebilde mit milder Spasshaftigkeit bemächtigen . . . " *Schriften*, VI, xxi.

[9] *Schriften*, I, xii ff.

[10] *Shakespeare*, p. 372.

[11] "Hatte ich früher die Schilderung der Leidenschaft, Kenntniss des Herzens und aller menschlichen Verirrungen und Gebrechen . . . vielleicht zu hoch angeschlagen, so begeisterte jetzt das Totale, die Anmuth und der Scherz, die tiefsinnige Weisheit der Erfindung und jener muthwillige Wahnsinn, der oft die selbst erfundenen Gesetze wieder vernichtet, meinen Sinn und meine Forschung, und das Spiel der Kunst, der edle Leichtsinn der Freude verdunkelte mir wohl auf Momente wieder die Grösse der Leidenschaft, die Schilderung des tiefen Seelenschmerzes in Shakspeare und Sophokles." *Schriften*, VI, xx; my italics in translation. This passage clearly illustrates the three phases in Tieck's critical thought: the early interest in objective psychological portrayal, the reaction in favor of a subjective expression of lighthearted joy, and finally the turning of his interest back toward the portrayal of tragic passion.

[12] See *Shakespeare*, pp. 18 ff., 119, *et passim*.

[13] "Das Lächerliche, welches sich mit dem Verächtlichen verbindet, und welches so manche Dichter zur Verfolgung, und wo möglich Vernichtung, dieser oder jener sogenannten Thorheit . . . haben brauchen wollen, ist . . . gehässig und bitter . . . ; auch gestehe ich gern, dass ich diesen sogenannten Satirikern, besonders der neuern Zeiten, niemals Freude und Lust habe abgewinnen können, ich weiss auch nicht, ob ich eben bei ihren Darstellungen gelacht habe. . . . Wie unterschieden ist aber . . . die Lust der Freude, das Entzücken unsrer ganzen Seele, . . . wenn alle unsere Anschauungen und Erinnerungen in jenem wunderbaren Strudel der Wonne auf eine Zeit untergehn, welcher die Töne des Gelächters aus der Verborgenheit herauf erschallen lässt." *Schriften*, IV, 97 f.

[14] "Jene Unschuld des Komischen, . . . jenes leichte Berühren aller Gegenstände, jenes gemüthliche Spiel mit allen Wesen und ihren Gedanken und Empfindungen, welches . . . einer der herrlichsten Vorzüge Shakspears ist." *Schriften*, IV, 99 f.

[15] *Nachgelassene Schriften*, II, 39.

[16] *Schriften*, XIII, 282 f.

[17] *Nachgelassene Schriften*, II, 48.

[18] *Ibid.*, p. 39.

¹⁹ "Die Schildbürger waren eine so edelmüthige Nation, dass sie ihre Schaubühne zu nichts Anderm brauchen wollten, als nur zu einem Anhange des Lazareths, um sich darin zu bessern. Sie sahen ein, dass sie viele Fehler an sich hatten, und deshalb gingen sie in's Theater, um sich davon zu reinigen. Das Schauspiel war also nicht etwa nur ein Spiel der Phantasie, oder ein Ort, wo man die Zeit mit angenehmen Possen hinbrachte, sondern eine wahre Schule der Sitten. Die Schildbürger nahmen es auch so genau, dass sie die Stücke gar nicht ausstehen konnten, in denen sie etwa unverhoffterweise hatten lachen müssen . . ." *Schriften,* IX, 54 f.

²⁰ See above, p. 60.

²¹ *Schriften,* XIII, 289.

²² *Schriften,* IV, 96 f.

²³ See above, pp. 31 ff.

²⁴ "Der Ernst sucht endlich den Scherz, und wieder ermüdet der Scherz, und sucht den Ernst; doch . . . trägt man in beides zu viel Absicht und Vorsatz hinein, so ist es gar leicht um den wahren Ernst, so wie um die wahre Lustigkeit geschehen." *Schriften,* V, 285; my italics in translation.

²⁵ "Wo denkt Ihr denn hin? Nun ja, da sieht man Euch das rohe Zeitalter recht an, rührend ist's, zum Weinen, alles voller Prediger und Prinzen, und Bösewichter, und hoher edler Menschen." *Schriften,* X, 276.

²⁶ "In welcher Trunkenheit jauchzt unser Geist, wenn es ihm einst vergönnt ist, tausend wechselnde, bunte, schwebende, tanzende Gestalten zu erblicken, die stets erneut und verjüngt in ihm aufsteigen. Angerührt, angelacht von tausendfältiger Liebe wickelt die Seele sich in Lieder von allen Farben und jubelt himmelan, dass das träge alltägliche Leben sie lange nicht wieder findet.
"Wie ein goldner Funke ein Feuerwerk anzündet . . . , dass das trunkene Auge . . . den Strudel der wechselnden farbigen Flammen mit Entzücken betrachtet: so ist es mit den wankenden, glänzenden Bildern, die die Freude uns vorführt." *Schriften,* V, 336.

²⁷ *Ibid.,* p. 412.

²⁸ *Shakespeare,* p. 399. This is from the draft written around 1800, after Tieck had had time to assimilate some of the Schlegels' ideas.

²⁹ *Schriften,* XI, xxii f.

³⁰ See above, p. 47.

³¹ *Schriften,* XII, 155-354.

³² *Kritische Schriften,* I, 184.

³³ *Schriften,* XIII, 289.

³⁴ *Schriften,* V, 280, 282.

³⁵ See above, p. 36.

³⁶ *Shakespeare,* p. 399.

³⁷ *Schriften,* IV, 111 f.

³⁸ "Dass es einen Witz geben könne, der in sich selber spiele und sich damit beruhige, dass es möglich, ja nothwendig sei, die ganze Zeit und Alles, was darin geschieht, für ein scherzhaftes Spiel anzusehen, und dass der rechte Spass eben der sei, an gar keinen Ernst zu glauben, . . . konnte ihm natürlich nicht einfallen . . ." *Nachgelassene Schriften,* II, 48; my italics in translation.

³⁹ "Ich biete Ihnen heut an, so viel ich von dieser Art besitze, eine luftige Composition, die ganz Schaum und leichter Scherz ist, und die Sie nicht ernsthafter nehmen müssen, als sie gemeint ist; doch kann man wohl nicht leicht über das Theater scherzen, ohne zugleich über die Welt zu scherzen . . ." *Schriften,* V, 159; my italics in translation.

⁴⁰ "Dass die Phantasie in der Lust übertreibt, versteht sich von selbst, denn sonst wäre ihre Darstellung keine poetische . . ." *Ibid.,* pp. 281 f.

[41] "Denn wenn man mich und Andere würdig genug fände, lächerlich zu sein, wenn wird dem Publicum als Exempel dienen sollten, so durften wir uns gegen treffliche Zusätze, Hyperbeln, grosse schlagende Züge nicht sperren, weil sich ohne diese ein individuelles Bild unmöglich zu einem allgemeinen erheben lässt." *Nachgelassene Schriften*, II, 71 f.

[42] *Ibid.*, pp. 76-84. On the last ground Tieck deprecates even the satires of Juvenal and Swift (*Schriften*, VI, xxi f.).

[43] "Noch nie, als bis jetzt, ist eine Periode gewesen, in der sich die Welt mit allen ihren Bemühungen und Ereignissen selber parodirt. Ehemals war es genug, einen einzelnen Menschen, eine Staatseinrichtung satirisch zu behandeln, und selbst der verwegene Aristophanes, der weder Götter noch Menschen schont, ist nicht darauf gefallen, sein ganzes Zeitalter komisch zu präsentiren . . . Jetzt ist es aber so weit mit uns gekommen, dass wir über nichts, oder über alles lachen müssen . . ." *Kritische Schriften*, I, 154 f.

[44] *Ibid.*, p. 170; cf. also p. 178.

[45] *Shakespeare*, pp. 368 f.

[46] "Es ensteht nun die Frage, ob es nicht verschiedene Arten der Täuschung giebt, und ob nicht Kunstwerke existiren, bei denen Täuschung nicht die erste Bedingung, das Hauptgesetz ausmacht." *Shakespeare*, pp. 401 f., quotation from p. 402.

[47] ". . . mit der Entstehung des Theaters entsteht auch der Scherz über das Theater, wie wir schon im Aristophanes sehn; er kann es kaum unterlassen, sich selbst zu ironisiren . . . , weil auf der Zweiheit, der Doppelheit des menschlichen Geistes, dem wunderbaren Widerspruch in uns, die Basis der komischen Bühne ruht. Die wunderliche Absicht des Theaters, eine Geschichte in grösster Lebendigkeit vor uns hinzustellen, hat Shakspear mehr als einmal in der Tragödie ironisirt, wo er in diesem Augenblick sein Schauspiel für Wahrheit ausgiebt, und im Gegensatze dieser vom Theater das Theater selbst als Lüge und schwache Nachahmung herabsetzt. Er musste seiner Sache sehr gewiss sein, dass er jene Störung der Illusion nicht befürchtete, die fast alle neueren Lehrbücher der Kunst prophezeien, wenn im Theater des Theaters erwähnt wird." *Schriften*, V, 280 f.

[48] *Ibid.*, p. 438.

[49] See *Shakespeare*, pp. 20 ff., 360.

[50] *Ibid.*, pp. 22, 231, 303 f., 362.

[51] See his justification of the mask in the preface to *Das Ungeheuer und der verzauberte Wald*, mentioned above, p. 72 and note 125, ch. iv.

[52] See *Kritische Schriften*, I, 166, 170 ff., 225; *Schriften*, V, 437 ff.

[53] *Schriften*, IX, 55; see above, p. 88.

[54] *Schriften*, XIII, 283.

[55] ". . . so ist wohl ohne Zweifel eine Art der Poesie erlaubt, welche auch das beste Theater nicht brauchen kann, sondern in der Phantasie eine Bühne für die Phantasie erbaut, und Kompositionen versucht, die vielleicht zugleich lyrisch, episch und dramatisch sind, die einen Umfang gewinnen, welcher gewissermassen dem Roman untersagt ist, und sich Kühnheiten aneignen, die keinem andern dramatischen Gedichte ziemen." *Schriften*, IV, 360 f.; quotation from p. 361.

[56] "Gemein hat es mit diesem die Mischung des Komischen und Ernsten, die Mannichfaltigkeit der Begebenheiten und die Vorliebe für Gegenstände aus der reichen und poetischen vaterländischen Geschichte . . ." *Kritische Schriften*, I, 220.

[57] ". . . im spanischen ist das Tragische und Komische streng geschieden, und wenn auch oft die Ironie des Dichters über seinen wilden und leidenschaftlichen Scenen schwebt, so sind seine Figuren doch in der Leidenschaft durchaus poetisch und erhaben, dagegen der Engländer selbst dem Fluge der höchsten Leidenschaft gern etwas Seltsames beimischt, das an das

Komische grenzt und seine Ironie oft in den Mittelpunkt des Schmerzes und der Leiden legt . . ." *Ibid.*, pp. 220 ff.; quotation from p. 222. Cf. August Wilhelm Schlegel's discussion of romantic comedy above, p. 39.

58 See Anneliese Bodensohn, *Ludwig Tiecks "Kaiser Oktavian" als romantische Dichtung*, Frankfurter Quellen und Forschungen zur germanischen und romanischen Philologie, XX (Frankfurt a. M., 1937), and Ernst Lüdtke, *Ludwig Tiecks "Kaiser Octavianus"* (diss. Greifswald, 1925).

59 *Tieck and Solger, the Complete Correspondence*, ed. P. Matenko, pp. 106 and 314.

60 For an analysis and historical exposition of the philosophical, psychological, and moral irony of *William Lovell*, see Fritz Brüggemann, *Die Ironie als entwicklungsgeschichtliches Moment* (Jena, 1909), pp. 1-26, 345-478.

61 "So oft sich der Philosoph verwundern muss, so oft er ein Ding nicht begreift, . . . eben so oft ruft er aus: darin ist kein Verstand!

"Ja der Verstand, wenn er sich recht auf den Grund kommen will, wenn er sein eignes Wesen bis ins Innerste erforscht, und sich nun selbst beobachtet und beobachtend vor sich liegen hat, sagt: darin ist kein Verstand." *Schriften*, V, 373.

62 *Kritische Schriften*, I, 172.

63 *Ludwig Tieck und die Brüder Schlegel: Briefe*, ed. H. Lüdeke (Frankfurt a. M., 1930), p. 151.

64 In the 253rd *Athenäum-Fragment*, Minor, II, 245; cf. also "Schlegel's Poetic Irony," *GR*, XXVI, 186.

65 Solger himself confirms this by praising the depth of irony manifested in the destiny of Andalosia, the hero of the second tragedy. *Tieck and Solger*, p. 340.

66 See "Schlegel's Poetic Irony," pp. 182 f., and ch. iii, above, pp. 43 f.

67 See the previously cited article by Oskar Walzel, "Methode? Ironie bei Fr. Schlegel und bei Solger," *Helicon*, I (1938), 33-50.

68 See the expositions of Solger's irony in his dialogue *Erwin* (Berlin, 1815), II, 276 ff., and in *Solger's Nachgelassene Schriften und Briefwechsel*, ed. Ludwig Tieck and Friedrich von Raumer (Leipzig, 1826), II, 561 ff. (The latter passage takes sharp issue with A. W. Schlegel's interpretation of Shakespearean irony, but the difference concerns the underlying spirit and philosophy of the dramatist; there is little disagreement on the concrete manifestations of irony in his works.) Cf. chapter six of Matenko's introduction, in *Tieck and Solger*, pp. 38-63; Fritz Ernst, *Die romantische Ironie* (diss. Zürich, 1915), pp. 33 ff.; Erich Schönebeck, *Tieck und Solger* (diss. Berlin, 1910), pp. 11 ff.

69 "Hier also wurde nun die ganz einfache Ironie, die Umkehrung der Sache, dass das Schlechte gut, und das Gute schlecht genannt wird, . . . völlig . . . missverstanden . . . Wie soll denn die höhere Ironie des Aristophanes, oder gar des Shakspear, . . . gefasst werden? Oder was sollen Leser . . . mit der sokratischen, oder jener Ironie anfangen, die Solger als jedem Kunstwerk unerlässlich verkündigt hat . . . ? Ueber dem Ganzen eines platonischen Dialogs (nehmen wir nur das Gastmal,) schwebt doch wohl noch eine höhere geistigere Ironie, als sich etwa in Sokrates scheinbarer Unwissenheit verkündigt. Und wie wollen denn Kritiker oder Philosophen jene letzte Vollendung eines poetischen Kunstwerks, die Gewähr . . . der ächten Begeisterung, jenen Aethergeist, der, so sehr er das Werk bis in seine Tiefen hinab mit Liebe durchdrang, doch befriedigt und unbefangen über dem Ganzen schwebt, und es von dieser Höhe nur, (so wie der Geniessende) erschaffen und fassen kann, nennen? Wenn wir diese Vollendung nicht mit Solger, oder mit Fr. Schlegel (wie dieser es früher im Athenäum schon andeutete) Ironie nennen sollen, so gebe und erfinde der Einsichtige einen andern Namen." *Schriften*, VI, xxvii ff.

[70] "Die Ironie, von der ich spreche, ist ja nicht Spott, Hohn, Persiflage, . . . es ist vielmehr der tiefste Ernst, der zugleich mit Scherz und wahrer Heiterkeit verbunden ist. . . . Sie ist die Kraft, die dem Dichter die Herrschaft über den Stoff erhält; er soll sich nicht an denselben verlieren, sondern über ihm stehen. So bewahrt ihn die Ironie vor Einseitigkeiten und leerem Idealisiren." Rudolf Köpke, *Ludwig Tieck. Erinnerungen aus dem Leben des Dichters* (Leipzig, 1855), II, 238 f.

[71] Minor, II, 187 ff., 211, 253. Cf. above, pp. 12 f., 19 ff. Cf. also Walzel, "Methode?," pp. 35 ff.

[72] "In meinen eigenen Dichtungen ist daher die Ironie zuerst mehr unbewusst, aber doch entschieden ausgedrückt; vor allem ist dies im *Lovell* der Fall. Die direkte Ironie herrscht im *Gestiefelten Kater*, von der höhern findet sich etwas im *Blaubart*, und entschieden ist sie im *Fortunat.*" Köpke, II, 174.

[73] *Ibid.*, pp. 217 ff., 239; cf. "Schlegel's Poetic Irony," pp. 185 f.

[74] Köpke, II, 218 ff., 239.

[75] "Aristophanes . . . durfte alle Bestrebungen seiner Umgebung . . . lächerlich und verwerflich finden, indem er jeden Unglauben und die Sophisterei seiner Tage verspottete, um der Gottesverehrung, dem Bürgersinn, der Vaterlandsliebe im Kämpfen Platz zu gewinnen. . . . Seine Begeisterung reisst uns mit auf die Höhe, auf welcher er selber steht, und von hier zeigt sich die Welt und ihr Bestreben läppisch und abgeschmackt, verderbt und elend, und doch gehen alle diese Empfindungen so in Unschuld und Wohlbehagen auf, dass die Polemik, die Erniedrigung des Menschen uns nicht verwundet und peinigt, sondern wir uns durch die Kunst des Dichters in einem wahrhaft beseligten Zustande befinden. Durch die Gewalt dieser ächten Ironie wird das Feindselige selbst in der Gestalt der Thorheit und des Unsinnes uns befreundet, und der begeisterte Dichter nimmt auch in sein lustiges Bild zum Theil die Bilder und Gesinnungen auf, für welche er kämpft, und lacht im glücklichsten Behagen auch über den Ernst, die Tugend und die Götter . . . , ohne dass in dieser durch und durch heitern Fröhlichkeit die Würde dieser Gegenstände vernichtet würde." *Kritische Schriften*, II, 322 f.

NOTES FOR CHAPTER SIX

[1] *Ehrenpforte und Triumphbogen für den Theaterpräsidenten von Kotzebue*, Böcking, II, 257-342.

[2] See note 18, ch. iv, above.

[3] When Friedrich Schlegel came to Berlin, Tieck was visiting in Hamburg, and he had not returned by late August. See *Friedrich Schlegels Briefe an seinen Bruder August Wilhelm*, ed. O. Walzel (Berlin, 1890), p. 293 [*FSAW*]; cf. also E. H. Zeydel, "Die ersten Beziehungen Ludwig Tiecks zu den Brüdern Schlegel," *JEGPh*, XXVII (1928), 16-41, and H. Lüdeke, *Ludwig Tieck und die Brüder Schlegel*, p. 19.

[4] See *FSAW*, p. 295 and editor's footnote 1.

[5] See Lüdeke, *op. cit.*, pp. 19 f.

[6] A. W. Schlegel emphasizes this ignorance of the authorship in a note added to the review in 1801. Böcking, XI, 143 f.

[7] "Die komische Laune, womit diess . . . Märchen dramatisiert ist, bleibt nicht in den Schranken des Gegenstandes stehen. Es spielt in der wirklichen Welt, ja mitten unter uns, und was nur bei Aufführung des Stücks . . . vorgeht, ist mit auf den Schauplatz gezogen, so dass man das Ganze . . . das Schauspiel eines Schauspieles nennen könnte. Es ist zu befürchten, dass es den Theoretikern viel Noth machen wird, die Gattung zu bestimmen, wohin es eigentlich gehört. So viel sieht man . . . ein, dass es eine Posse ist, eine kecke, muthwillige Posse, worin der Dichter sich alle Augenblicke selbst zu unterbrechen und sein eignes Werk zu zerstören scheint, um nur

desto mehr Spöttereien . . . nach allen Seiten wie leichte Pfeile fliegen zu lassen. Doch geschieht diess mit so viel fröhlicher Gutmüthigkeit, dass man es ergötzlich finden müsste, wenn auch unsre eignen Vettern und Basen lächerlich gemacht sein sollten. Wer also etwa durch die Lustspiele, die man auf unsern Theatern giebt, in eine zu ernsthafte Stimmung gerathen ist, dem können diese Thorheiten als ein gutes Gegenmittel dienen." Böcking, XI, 141; my italics in translation.

[8] "Man sieht, es geht ziemlich bunt durcheinander: wenn es den Verfasser nur nicht einmal gereut, sich und Andre unterhalten zu haben! Denn —verstehn wir ihn anders recht—so hätte er sich gar über das Publikum selbst lustig gemacht. Nun nahm es zwar, wie bekannt, das heilige Volk von Athen sehr geneigt auf, wenn man es von der Bühne herunter zum Besten hatte: aber nicht alle Nationen besitzen in gleichem Grade die Gabe Spass zu verstehn . . . Dem sei wie ihm wolle: da das Publikum nicht in Person das Empfangene vergelten kann, so mögen es diejenigen thun, mit welchen sich Peter Leberecht besonders in den Stand des Krieges gesetzt hat. Doch sei Scherz die Waffe, denn mit Ernst ist solch ein Dämon nicht wegzubannen." *Ibid.*, p. 143; my italics in translation.

[9] See above, p. 37.

[10] See above, pp. 30 f. However, as early as December, 1796, he recommended modern "adaptations of the ancient comic and satiric poets" to Johann Daniel Falk (*Briefe von und an A. W. Schlegel*, ed. Josef Körner [Zürich, Leipzig, Wien, 1930], I, 48). Ironically enough, Falk followed the advice by some polemic satire against the Romanticists, in return for which he was caricatured by Tieck in *Anti-Faust*.

[11] "Die Recension des Tieck . . . hat mir wegen der klassischen *Grazie* und Urbanität grosse Freude gemacht; obgleich ich Tieck weit mehr wegen des Lovell und seine [sic] Person schätze als des Katers wegen, den ich nicht reich, nicht frech und nicht poetisch genung finde. Das letzte hast Du, wo ich Dich verstehe, auch angedeutet. Er giebts auch zu." *FSAW*, p. 306; italics represent spaced type. Actually, there is nothing in August Wilhelm's review to intimate any dissatisfaction on his part with *Der gestiefelte Kater*.

[12] "Wer also einiges Bedürfniss für alle diese Dinge hat, wird sich gern von jener materiellen Masse, jener breiten Natürlichkeit zu luftigeren Bildungen der Phantasie wenden, die bald heitern Scherz hingaukeln, bald die Musik zarter Regungen anklingen lassen. Ihm wird alsdann eine ruhige Darstellung sehr erquickend entgegen kommen, die, wenn sie auch noch nicht bis zur Vollendung gediehen ist, doch in der milden Temperatur eines künstlerischen Sinnes geboren wurde. . . . In einer Erzählung der Mutter Gans das leibhaftige deutsche Theater sammt allem Zubehör aufs Theater zu bringen, ist wahrlich unerhört. Wenn die Satire noch methodisch, deklamatorisch, gallicht wäre; aber grade umgekehrt, sie ist durchaus muthwillig und possenhaft, kurz gegen alle rechtliche Ordnung. Ich gebe den Verfasser verloren: er wird sich niemals von den Streichen, die er ausgetheilt hat, erholen können. . . . Diess sind ungefähr die Schalkheiten, die sich unter dem ehrsamen Titel Volksmärchen . . . eingedrängt haben. Kann ihnen die unbesonnene Leichtigkeit, womit sie in die Welt gesprungen sind, keine Verzeihung auswirken; . . . so wird man sie wenigstens über der kindlichen Unbefangenheit, womit die übrigen Stücke behandelt sind, vergessen." Böcking, XII, 27 ff.; my italics in translation.

[13] *Ibid.*, p. 36.

[14] *Ibid.*, p. 32.

[15] August Wilhelm suggests that *Blaubart* is ironic in the sense of Friedrich Schlegel's 51st *Athenäum-Fragment* (see p. 12, above) when he notes its alternating effects of circumspection and lively sympathy (*Besonnenheit, lebhaftere Teilnahme*) upon the reader. *Ibid.*, p. 33.

[16] "Unter seinen andern *Volksmährchen* gefallen mir mehre besser als die dramatischen Sachen." *FSAW*, p. 310.

[17] "Aber der Sternbald vereinigt den Ernst und Schwung des Lovell mit der künstlerischen Religiosität des Klosterbruders und mit allem was in den poetischen Arabesken, die er aus alten Mährchen gebildet, im Ganzen genommen das Schönste ist: die fantastische Fülle und Leichtigkeit, der Sinn für Ironie, und besonders die absichtliche Verschiedenheit und Einheit des Kolorits. Auch hier ist alles klar und transparent, und der romantische Geist scheint angenehm über sich selbst zu fantasiren." Minor, II, 278 f.; my italics in translation.

[18] *FSAW*, p. 414. This letter dates from early 1799; *Sternbald* had appeared in 1798, one year after *Der gestiefelte Kater.*

[19] "Das Werk soll *Romantische und Dramatische Darstellung* heissen . . . Eigentlich ists nichts anders, als eine Fortsetzung der Volksmährchen. . . . Ausser dem, was Du aus eigner Erfahrung über die Ausgezeichnetheit des Einzelnen zu seiner Empfehlung sagen wirst, kannst Du auch noch *auf mein Wort* (um so mehr, da er mir sehr viele Plane gesagt, auch eine Probe vorgelesen hat) die *grösste Mannichfaltigkeit* versprechen. Wenn Du die Volksmährchen und den Lovell nun schon gelesen hast: so ist meine Erinnrung überflüssig." *Ibid.*, pp. 311 f.; italics represent spaced type. In a footnote on p. 311 Walzel identifies the work as *Prinz Zerbino* or the collection to which this play belongs. Later August Wilhelm read the proofs of *Zerbino* with "delight," and Friedrich thought of emulating the personal satire of the "classic" Allegorical Mill. See Holtei, *Briefe an Ludwig Tieck,* III, 229; *Caroline, Briefe aus der Frühromantik,* ed. Erich Schmidt (Leipzig, 1913), I, 501.

[20] "Mancher der vortrefflichsten Romane ist ein Compendium, eine Encyclopädie des ganzen geistigen Lebens eines genialischen Individuums; Werke die das sind, selbst in ganz andrer Form, wie Nathan, bekommen dadurch einen Anstrich von Roman. . . ." Minor, II, 194 (78th *Lyceum-Fragment*).

[21] "Die romantische Poesie ist eine progressive Universalpoesie. Ihre Bestimmung ist nicht bloss, alle getrennte Gattungen der Poesie wieder zu vereinigen . . . Sie will, und soll auch Poesie und Prosa, Genialität und Kritik, Kunstpoesie und Naturpoesie bald mischen, bald verschmelzen, . . . die Formen der Kunst mit gediegnem Bildungsstoff jeder Art anfüllen und sättigen, und durch die Schwingungen des Humors beseelen. . . . Die romantische Dichtart ist die einzige, die mehr als Art, und gleichsam die Dichtkunst selbst ist: denn in einem gewissen Sinn ist oder soll alle Poesie romantisch seyn." Minor, II, 220 f. On the relation of *romantic* poetry to the *Roman,* which appears to be stressed in this *Fragment,* see Arthur O. Lovejoy, "The Meaning of 'Romantic' in Early German Romanticism," in his *Essays in the History of Ideas* (Baltimore, 1948), pp. 183-206; as Lovejoy demonstrates, the *romantic* connoted for Friedrich Schlegel the expansive, heterogeneous style which he associated with medieval and early modern literature in general, not the *Roman* as a *genre.*

[22] "Wenn ich meine Antipathie gegen das Katzengeschlecht erkläre, so nehme ich Peter Leberechts gestiefelten Kater aus. Krallen hat er, und wer davon geritzt worden ist, schreyt, wie billig, über ihn; Andre aber kann es belustigen, wie er gleichsam auf dem Dache der dramatischen Kunst herumspaziert." Minor, II, 254. This was the metaphor which Haym converted into a "symbol of irony" (see the opening paragraph of the present study).

[23] *FSAW*, p. 379.

[24] "Was Du über Tieck geschrieben, gefällt mir ausnehmend gut. Der Gesichtspunkt ist sehr bestimmt und ich finde es nicht zu viel." *FSAW*, p. 388.

[25] *Briefe von und an Friedrich und Dorothea Schlegel,* ed. Josef Körner (Berlin, 1926), p. 39.

26 "Tiecks reifere Werke, den Sternbald, die Genoveva, den Octavian, den Phantasus mit aller darin enthaltenen Mannichfaltigkeit, die Novellen, den . . . Krieg der Cevennen, kann man nicht nach ihrem wahren Werth und Gehalt würdigen, ohne in die innersten Geheimnisse der Poesie einzugehn. . . ." Böcking, XI, 145.

27 See note 17, above, where the pertinent concluding sentences are quoted in full.

28 See above, pp. 105 f., and note 16.

29 See "Schlegel's Poetic Irony," *GR*, XXVI, 185 ff.

30 *Nachgelassene Schriften*, II, 39.

31 See above, p. 104.

32 "Seltener glaubte ich darin einen von den zerstreuten Zauberklängen in Shakspeares Liedern zu hören. Überhaupt würde man, wie mir däucht, Ihre innige Vertrautheit mit diesem Dichter weniger vermuthen. Vielleicht kommt es nur daher, weil Sie noch nichts in Shakspeares Form dramatisirt haben. Ein romantisch-komisches Schauspiel, der ernsthafte Theil in fünf-füssigen Jamben, auch wohl mit untermischten Reimen, nur der komische Dialog in Prosa, das müsste Ihnen herrlich gelingen." *Ludwig Tieck und die Brüder Schlegel*, ed. H. Lüdeke, pp. 33 f.

33 *Tieck and Solger*, p. 335.

34 ". . . es war in Deutschland vom Charakter des Romantischen so viel die Rede gewesen, und vom Calderon für die allegorische Poesie begeistert, versuchte ich es in diesem wundersamen Mährchen zugleich meine Ansicht der romantischen Poesie allegorisch, lyrisch und dramatisch niederzulegen." *Schriften*, I, xxxviii.

NOTES FOR CONCLUSION

1 Maurice Boucher, in *Le Romantisme allemand*, ed. Albert Béguin ([Paris], Les Cahiers du Sud, 1949), pp. 28 ff.

2 *Ibid.*, p. 28.

3 Quoted by Newman I. White, *Shelley* (New York, 1940), I, 509. Shelley himself applies standards like those of Tieck in condemning the drama of the Restoration: "At such periods the calculating principle pervades all the forms of dramatic exhibition, and poetry ceases to be expressed upon them. Comedy loses its ideal universality: wit succeeds to humor; we laugh from self-complacency and triumph, instead of pleasure; malignity, sarcasm, and contempt, succeed to sympathetic merriment; we hardly laugh, but we smile." "A Defence of Poetry," *Shelley's Literary and Philosophical Criticism*, ed. John Shawcross (London, 1909), p. 136.

BIBLIOGRAPHICAL REFERENCES

I. *Sources*

A. Tieck:

Tieck, Ludwig. *Schriften.* 28 vols. Berlin: G. Reimer, 1828-54.

———. *Kritische Schriften.* 4 vols. Leipzig: F. A. Brockhaus, 1848-52.

———. *Nachgelassene Schriften,* ed. R. Köpke. 2 vols. in 1. Leipzig: F. A. Brockhaus, 1855.

———. *Das Buch über Shakespeare,* ed. H. Lüdeke. Neudrucke deutscher Literaturwerke des 18. und 19. Jahrhunderts, I. Halle, 1920. Pp. xxvi + 524. Cited in the notes as *Shakespeare.*

———. *Der gestiefelte Kater,* in *Satiren und Parodien,* ed. Andreas Müller. Deutsche Literatur. Reihe Romantik, IX (Leipzig, 1935), 13-62, with editor's notes, pp. 236 f. Cited in the notes as *GK.*

———. *Puss in Boots,* trans. Lillie Winter, in *The German Classics of the Nineteenth and Twentieth Centuries,* ed. Kuno Francke, IV (Albany, n. d.), 194-251. Cited in the notes as *PB.*

Köpke, Rudolf. *Ludwig Tieck. Erinnerungen aus dem Leben des Dichters nach dessen mündlichen und schriftlichen Mittheilungen.* 2 vols. Leipzig: F. A. Brockhaus, 1855.

B. August Wilhelm Schlegel:

Schlegel, August Wilhelm von. *Sämmtliche Werke,* ed. E. Böcking. 12 vols. Leipzig: Weidmann'sche Buchhandlung, 1846-47.

———. *Vorlesungen über schöne Litteratur und Kunst,* ed. J. Minor. 3 vols. Deutsche Litteraturdenkmale des 18. und 19. Jahrhunderts, XVII-XIX. Heilbronn, 1884.

———. *Vorlesungen über Philosophische Kunstlehre mit erläuternden Bemerkungen von Karl Christian Friedrich Krause,* ed. A. Wünsche. Leipzig: Dieterichsche Verlagshandlung, 1911. Pp. iv + 371.

———. *Vorlesungen über dramatische Kunst und Literatur,* ed. G. V. Amoretti. 2 vols. Bonn and Leipzig: K. Schroeder, 1923.

C. Friedrich Schlegel:

Schlegel, Friedrich. *Sämmtliche Werke.* 2nd ed. 15 vols. in 7. Wien: I. Klang, 1846.

———. *Seine prosaischen Jugendschriften,* ed. J. Minor. 2 vols. in 1, Wien: C. Konegen, 1882. Cited in the notes as Minor.

D. Correspondence Among the Early German Romanticists:

Briefe an Ludwig Tieck, ed. Karl von Holtei. 4 vols. in 2. Breslau: E. Trewendt, 1864.

Wackenroder, Wilhelm Heinrich. "Briefwechsel mit Ludwig Tieck," *Werke und Briefe,* ed. F. von der Leyen. Jena, 1910. II, 1-199.

Ludwig Tieck und die Brüder Schlegel. Briefe mit Einleitung und Anmerkungen, ed. H. Lüdeke. Ottendorfer Memorial Fellowship Series of New York University, XIII. Frankfurt a. M.: J. Baer, 1930. Pp. 252.

Tieck and Solger. The Complete Correspondence, ed. Percy Matenko. New York and Berlin: B. Westermann, 1933. Pp. xvi + 593.

Letters of Ludwig Tieck, Hitherto Unpublished, ed. E. H. Zeydel, P. Matenko, and R. H. Fife. New York: MLA; London: Oxford University Press, 1937. Pp. xxxi + 604.

Friedrich Schlegels Briefe an seinen Bruder August Wilhelm, ed. O. F. Walzel. Berlin: Speyer & Peters, 1890. Pp. xxvi + 680. Cited in the notes as *FSAW*.

Caroline, Briefe aus der Frühromantik, ed. Erich Schmidt. 2 vols. Leipzig: Insel, 1913.

Briefe von und an Friedrich und Dorothea Schlegel, ed. J. Körner. Berlin: Askanischer Verlag, 1926. Pp. vii + 727.

Briefe von und an August Wilhelm Schlegel, ed. J. Körner. 2 vols. Zürich, Leipzig, Wien: Amalthea, 1930.

E. Other Authors:

Aristophanes. With the English Translation of Benjamin B. Rogers. 3 vols. The Loeb Classical Library. London: W. Heinemann; New York: G. P. Putnam's Sons, 1924.

Lessing, Gotthold Ephraim. *Sämtliche Schriften*, ed. K. Lachmann and F. Muncker. 3rd edition. 23 vols. in 24. Stuttgart: Göschen, 1886-1924.

Schikaneder, Emanuel. *Die Zauberflöte*, in *Die Maschinenkomödie*, ed. O. Rommel. Deutsche Literatur. Reihe Barock: Barocktradition im österreichisch-bayrischen Volkstheater, I, 263-318.

Schiller, Friedrich. *Sämtliche Werke, Säkular-Ausgabe*, ed. E. von der Hellen. 16 vols. Stuttgart and Berlin: Cotta [1904-5].

Solger, Karl Wilhelm Ferdinand. *Erwin. Vier Gespräche über das Schöne und die Kunst.* 2 vols. in 1. Berlin: Realschulbuchhandlung, 1815.

——. *Ibid.* Ed. Rudolf Kurtz. Berlin: Wiegandt & Grieben, 1907. Pp. xxx + 396.

——. *Nachgelassene Schriften und Briefwechsel*, ed. L. Tieck and Fr. v. Raumer. 2 vols. Leipzig: F. A. Brockhaus, 1826.

Weise, Christian. *Lustspiel von der verkehrten Welt. Neue Jugend-, Lust-: Das ist Drey Schauspiele.* Frankfurt and Leipzig, 1684. III.

II. *Critical Literature*

A. Works on Tieck:

Bertrand, J.-J. A. *L. Tieck et le théâtre espagnol.* Paris: F. Rieder, 1914. Pp. 182.

Bischoff, Heinrich. *Ludwig Tieck als Dramaturg.* Bibliothèque de la Faculté de philosophie et lettres de l'Université de Liège, II. Bruxelles, 1897. Pp. 124.

Bodensohn, Anneliese. *Ludwig Tiecks "Kaiser Oktavian" als romantische Dichtung.* Frankfurter Quellen und Forschungen zur germanischen und romanischen Philologie, XX. Frankfurt a. M., 1937. Pp. 96.

Brodnitz, Käthe. *Die vier Märchenkomödien von Ludwig Tieck.* Diss. München, 1912. Pp. 101.

Brüggemann, Fritz. *Die Ironie als entwicklungsgeschichtliches Moment.* Jena: E. Diederichs, 1909. Pp. viii + 478.

Budde, Josef. *Zur romantischen Ironie bei Ludwig Tieck.* Diss. Bonn, 1907. Pp. 32.

Faerber, Ludwig. *Das Komische bei Ludwig Tieck.* Diss. Giessen, 1917. Pp. 88.

Frerking, J. "Zwei Shakespeareparodien in Tiecks 'Verkehrter Welt,'" *Euphorion*, XVII (1910), 355 f.

Gentges, Ignaz. "Tiecks Märchenbühne," *Das deutsche Theater: Jahrbuch für Drama und Bühne*, I (Bonn and Leipzig, 1922-23), 144-160.

Görte, Erna. *Der junge Tieck und die Aufklärung.* Germanische Studien, XLV. Berlin, 1926. Pp. 102.

Günther, H. *Romantische Kritik und Satire bei Ludwig Tieck.* Diss. Leipzig, 1907. Pp. 213.

Hewett-Thayer, Harvey W. "Tieck's Revision of His Satirical Comedies," *GR*, XII (1937), 147-164.

Immerwahr, Raymond M. "Ludwig Tieck's Contribution in Theory and Practice to the German Romanticists' Conception of Comedy." Diss. University of California, Berkeley, 1941. Pp. 372.

Jost, Walter. *Von Ludwig Tieck zu E. T. A. Hoffmann.* Deutsche Forschungen, IV. Frankfurt a. M., 1921. Pp. x + 138.

Kaiser, Oskar. *Der Dualismus Ludwig Tiecks als Dramatiker und Dramaturg.* Diss. Leipzig, 1885. Pp. 67.

Lieske, Rudolf. *Tiecks Abwendung von der Romantik.* Germanische Studien, CXXXIV. Berlin, 1933. Pp. 150.

Lüdeke, Henry. *Ludwig Tieck und das alte englische Theater.* Deutsche Forschungen, VI. Frankfurt a. M., 1922. Pp. viii + 373.

Lüdtke, Ernst. *Ludwig Tiecks "Kaiser Octavianus."* Diss. Greifswald, 1925. Pp. 236.

Lussky, Alfred E. *Tieck's Romantic Irony. With Special Emphasis Upon the Influence of Cervantes, Sterne, and Goethe.* Chapel Hill: University of North Carolina Press, 1932. Pp. viii + 274.

Minder, Robert. *Un Poète romantique allemand: Ludwig Tieck (1773-1853).* Publications de la faculté des lettres de l'Université de Strasbourg, LXXII [1936]. Pp. viii + 516.

Pfeiffer, Emilie. *Shakespeares und Tiecks Märchendramen.* Mnemosyne, XIII. Bonn, 1933. Pp. 84.

Riederer, F. *Ludwig Tiecks Beziehungen zur deutschen Literatur des 17. Jahrhunderts.* Diss. Greifswald, 1915. Pp. 125.

Rosenkranz, Karl. "Ludwig Tieck und die romantische Schule," in *Studien zur Philosophie und Literatur.* Leipzig [1848]. IV, 277-344.

Schönebeck, Erich. *Tieck und Solger.* Diss. Berlin, 1910. Pp. 87.

Stanger, Hermann. "Der Einfluss Ben Jonsons auf Ludwig Tieck," *Studien zur vergleichenden Litteraturgeschichte,* I (1901), 182-227; II (1902), 37-86.

Wolf, Jacques. "Les Allusions politiques dans le 'Chat botté' de Ludwig Tieck," *Revue germanique,* V (1909), 158-201.

Zeydel, Edwin H. "Die ersten Beziehungen L. Tiecks zu den Brüdern Schlegel," *JEGPh,* XXVII (1928), 16-41.

———. "Das Reh — ein Jugendwerk Ludwig Tiecks," *Euphorion,* XXIX (1928), 93-108.

———. *Ludwig Tieck and England.* Princeton, 1931. Pp. vii + 263.

———. *Ludwig Tieck, the German Romanticist.* Princeton, 1935. Pp. xvi + 406.

B. Works on German Romanticism:

Béguin, Albert, ed. *Le Romantisme allemand. Textes et études.* [Paris]: Les Cahiers du Sud, 1949. Pp. 493.

Ernst, Fritz. *Die romantische Ironie.* Diss. Zürich, 1915. Pp. 130 + xxvii.

Gundolf, Friedrich. *Romantiker.* Berlin-Wilmersdorf: H. Keller, 1930. Pp. 395.

———. *Romantiker: Neue Folge.* Berlin-Wilmersdorf: H. Keller, 1931. Pp. 255.

Haym, Rudolf. *Die Romantische Schule,* 4th edition, ed. O. F. Walzel. Berlin: Weidmann, 1920. Pp. xii + 994.

Hettner, Hermann. *Die romantische Schule in ihrem inneren Zusammen- hange mit Goethe und Schiller.* Braunschweig: Vieweg, 1850. Pp. vi + 207.

Huch, Ricarda. *Die Romantik: Ausbreitung, Blütezeit und Verfall.* Tübingen and Stuttgart: R. Wunderlich, 1951. Pp. 675.

Immerwahr, Raymond. "The Subjectivity or Objectivity of Friedrich Schlegel's Poetic Irony," *GR,* XXVI (1951), 173-191. Cited in the notes as "Schlegel's Poetic Irony."

Joachimi[-Dege], Marie. *Die Weltanschauung der deutschen Romantik.* Jena and Leipzig: E. Diederichs, 1905. Pp. viii + 237. Cited in the notes as *Weltanschauung.*

——. *Deutsche Shakespeare-Probleme im XVIII. Jahrhundert und im Zeitalter der Romantik.* Untersuchungen zur neueren Sprach- und Literaturgeschichte, XII. Leipzig, 1907. Pp. ix + 296. Cited in the notes as *Probleme.*

Lovejoy, Arthur O. "The Meaning of 'Romantic' in Early German Roman- ticism" and "Schiller and the Genesis of German Romanticism," in *Essays in the History of Ideas.* Baltimore: Johns Hopkins Press, 1948. Pp. 183-227.

Münnig, Elisabeth von. *Calderón und die ältere deutsche Romantik.* Berlin: Mayer & Müller, 1912. Pp. 88.

Röhl, Hans. *Die ältere Romantik und die Kunst des jungen Goethe.* For- schungen zur neueren Literaturgeschichte, XXXVI. Berlin, 1909. Pp. x + 164.

Silz, Walter. *Early German Romanticism. Its Founders and Heinrich von Kleist.* Cambridge, Mass.: Harvard University Press, 1929. Pp. xi + 264.

Tumarkin, Anna. *Die romantische Weltanschauung.* Bern: P. Haupt, 1920. Pp. 147.

Ulshöfer, Robert. *Die Theorie des Dramas in der deutschen Romantik.* Neue deutsche Forschungen, XXIX. Berlin, 1935. Pp. 183.

Walzel, Oskar F., ed. *August Wilhelm und Friedrich Schlegel.* Deutsche National-Litteratur, CXLIII. Stuttgart [1891-92]. Pp. i-lxxv.

——. "Schiller und die Romantik," in *Vom Geistesleben des 18. und 19. Jahrhunderts.* Leipzig: Insel, 1911. Pp. 63-94.

——. *Deutsche Romantik: II. Die Dichtung.* Aus Natur und Geisteswelt, CCXXXIII. 5th ed. Leipzig and Berlin: B. G. Teubner, 1926. Pp. 114.

——. *Romantisches.* Mnemosyne, XVIII. Bonn, 1934. Pp. 253.

——. "Methode? Ironie bei Fr. Schlegel und bei Solger," *Helicon,* I (1938), 33-50. Cited in the notes as "Methode?"

Wendriner, Karl Georg. *Das romantische Drama.* Berlin: Oesterheld, 1909. Pp. 168.

Wernaer, Robert M. *Romanticism and the Romantic School in Germany.* New York and London: D. Appleton, 1910. Pp. xv + 373.

C. Works on Comedy:

Beare, Mary. *Die Theorie der Komödie von Gottsched bis Jean Paul.* Diss. Bonn, 1927. Pp. 89.

Bergson, Henri. *Le Rire.* 8th ed. Paris: F. Alcan, 1912. Pp. vii + 204.

Bohtz, August Wilhelm. *Ueber das Komische und die Komödie.* Göttingen, 1844. Pp. vi + 266.

Gregory, J. C. *The Nature of Laughter.* New York and London: Harcourt, Brace, 1924. Pp. v + 241.

Güttinger, Fritz. *Die romantische Komödie und das deutsche Lustspiel.* Wege zur Dichtung, XXXIV. Frauenfeld and Leipzig: Huber, 1939. Pp. 273.

Hille, Curt. *Die deutsche Komödie unter der Einwirkung des Aristophanes.* Breslauer Beiträge zur Literaturgeschichte, XII. Leipzig, 1907. Pp. vi + 180.

Holl, Karl. *Geschichte des deutschen Lustspiels.* Leipzig: J. J. Weber, 1923. Pp. xv + 439.

Jernigan, Charlton C. *Incongruity in Aristophanes.* Diss. Duke University, 1939. Pp. 48.

Lipps, Theodor. *Komik und Humor.* Beiträge zur Aesthetik, VI. Hamburg and Leipzig, 1898. Pp. viii + 264.

Lord, Louis E. *Aristophanes: His Plays and His Influence.* Boston: M. Jones, 1925. Pp. xi + 183.

Pulver, Max. *Romantische Ironie und romantische Komödie.* Diss. Freiburg, 1912. Pp. 36.

Rusack, Hedwig H. *Gozzi in Germany.* Columbia University Germanic Studies. New York, 1930. Pp. xiii + 195.

Süss, Wilhelm. *Aristophanes und die Nachwelt.* Das Erbe der Alten, II-III. Leipzig: Dieterich, 1911. Pp. 226.

Walzel, Oskar F. "Aristophanische Komödien," *Zeitschrift für den deutschen Unterricht,* XXX (1916), 481-507.

INDEX

WASHINGTON UNIVERSITY STUDIES
(NEW SERIES)
LANGUAGE AND LITERATURE

WASHINGTON UNIVERSITY STUDIES
(NEW SERIES)

Early English and American Critics of French Symbolism
by Bruce A. Morrissette

Bibliographical Data on Diderot..by Herbert Dieckmann

Rosencrantz and Guildenstern..by W. Roy Mackenzie

The Contemporary Reception of Edmund Burke's Speaking
by Donald Cross Bryant

The Moral Sense of Simplicity..by Richard F. Jones

Imitation as an Aesthetic Norm..by Fred O. Nolte

Immediacy: Its Nature and Value..by Charles E. Cory

WASHINGTON UNIVERSITY STUDIES
(NEW SERIES)

SCIENCE AND TECHNOLOGY

WASHINGTON UNIVERSITY STUDIES
(NEW SERIES)

SOCIAL AND PHILOSOPHICAL SCIENCES

*Orders for any of these publications should be addressed to the Bookstore,
Washington University, St. Louis 5, Mo.*